SINGER SIMPLE

decorative machine stitching

essential machine-side tips and techniques

DISCARDED

the editors of SINGER Worldwide

Heather Brine Lambert has illustrated a variety of books and magazine articles over the past two decades. She also applies her artistic bent to interior and home design. Ms. Lambert resides in Massachusetts with her husband, Dave, daughters April and Kara, and an assortment of dogs and cats.

Creative Publishing
international

Copyright © 2008
Creative Publishing international, Inc.
400 First Avenue North
Suite 300
Minneapolis, MN 55401
1-800-328-3895
www.creativepub.com

ISBN-13: 978-1-58923-341-6
ISBN-10: 1-58923-341-7

10 9 8 7 6 5 4 3 2 1

Library of Congress Cataloging-in-Publication Data
Decorative machine stitching : essential machine-side tips and techniques / the editors of Singer Worldwide.
    p. cm. -- (Singer simple)
  Includes bibliographical references and index.
  ISBN 1-58923-341-7 (alk. paper)
  1. Machine sewing. 2. Fancy work. 3. Textile crafts. I. Creative Publishing International. II. Title.

TT713.D39 2008
646.2'044--dc22
                                        2007034376
                                        CIP

Associate Editor: Beth Baumgartel
Technical Editor: Carol Fresia
Copy Editor: Kristy Mulkern
Proofreader: Andrea Schein
Page Layout: Susan Gilday and Heather Brine Lambert
Illustrations: Heather Brine Lambert

Printed in China

contents

craving something special?

Here's the extra dazzle you need!

Maybe you don't think you're very creative. Or maybe you just don't know where to begin. *Singer Simple Decorative Machine Stitching* will teach you how to turn your ideas into beautiful stitches and plain fabrics into works of art. There are so many ways to get creative with stitches. Once you get started, you won't want to stop!

Whether you're stitching by hand or by sewing machine, embroidery machine, or serger, *Singer Simple Decorative Machine Stitching* is your essential guide. The color-coded pages teach you all the basics of thread embellishment, in a concise, step-by-step format, for easy reference. From the simplicity of the basic zigzag stitch to the intricacy of computer-generated embroidery motifs, *Singer Simple Decorative Machine Stitching* will inspire you to develop your own creative style.

All you need is an idea!

You don't need a computerized embroidery machine (although they are wonderful). Even the most basic sewing machines have some built-in decorative stitches—so check your manual. Whatever you do, start simple! You might want to stitch a motif in metallic thread on the back pocket of your favorite jeans. Or have some fun with glow-in-the-dark stitching on pajamas or color-changing thread on a terrycloth bib. It's so easy to express yourself in stitches!

Heather Brine Lambert has illustrated a variety of books and magazine articles over the past two decades. She also applies her artistic bent to interior and home design. Ms. Lambert resides in Massachusetts with her husband, Dave, daughters April and Kara, and an assortment of dogs and cats.

Creative Publishing
international

Copyright © 2008
Creative Publishing international, Inc.
400 First Avenue North
Suite 300
Minneapolis, MN 55401
1-800-328-3895
www.creativepub.com

ISBN-13: 978-1-58923-341-6
ISBN-10: 1-58923-341-7

10 9 8 7 6 5 4 3 2 1

Library of Congress Cataloging-in-Publication Data
Decorative machine stitching : essential machine-side tips and techniques / the editors of Singer Worldwide.
    p. cm. -- (Singer simple)
  Includes bibliographical references and index.
  ISBN 1-58923-341-7 (alk. paper)
 1. Machine sewing. 2. Fancy work. 3. Textile crafts. I. Creative Publishing International. II. Title.

TT713.D39 2008
646.2'044--dc22
                                        2007034376
                                            CIP

Associate Editor: Beth Baumgartel
Technical Editor: Carol Fresia
Copy Editor: Kristy Mulkern
Proofreader: Andrea Schein
Page Layout: Susan Gilday and Heather Brine Lambert
Illustrations: Heather Brine Lambert

Printed in China

choosing
a machine

Your machine is your most important tool, so you want to be sure to choose the one that best suits your interest and needs. There are three basic types of sewing machine. Which is right for you? Read on to learn more.

sewing machines: Regular sewing machines sew straight and zigzag stitches, with some built-in decorative stitches. They don't allow you to work hooped embroidery, but they do sew beautiful linear stitches.

Many sewing machines are computerized, which means they have a large library of stitches, and also allow you to edit, or modify, the stitches. If you're passionate about decorative stitching, invest in a computerized machine.

sewing/embroidery machines: These top-of-the-line machines have an embroidery module for sewing multicolor, hooped embroidery. They also have an internal computer that programs the stitching and allows you to edit designs. When the embroidery module is not attached, the machine works as a sewing-only model—with all the bells and whistles.

embroidery machines: These specialized machines stitch multicolor, motif-style hooped embroidery quickly and professionally. Keep in mind that they do not sew straight rows of stitches—they're designed only for embellishing.

If you already own a sewing machine but want to do more embroidery, this machine is an excellent tool for expanding your repertoire.

9

choosing a machine

Your machine is your most important tool, so you want to be sure to choose the one that best suits your interest and needs. There are three basic types of sewing machine. Which is right for you? Read on to learn more.

sewing machines: Regular sewing machines sew straight and zigzag stitches, with some built-in decorative stitches. They don't allow you to work hooped embroidery, but they do sew beautiful linear stitches.

Many sewing machines are computerized, which means they have a large library of stitches, and also allow you to edit, or modify, the stitches. If you're passionate about decorative stitching, invest in a computerized machine.

sewing/embroidery machines: These top-of-the-line machines have an embroidery module for sewing multicolor, hooped embroidery. They also have an internal computer that programs the stitching and allows you to edit designs. When the embroidery module is not attached, the machine works as a sewing-only model—with all the bells and whistles.

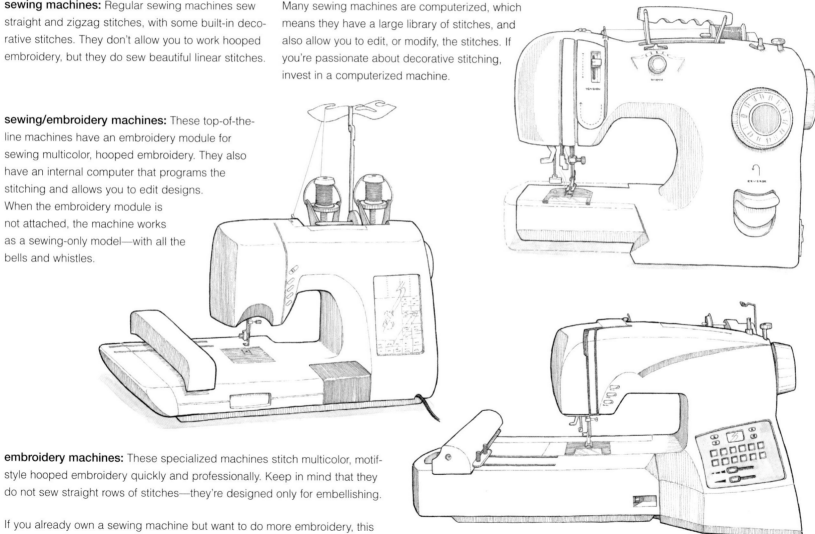

embroidery machines: These specialized machines stitch multicolor, motif-style hooped embroidery quickly and professionally. Keep in mind that they do not sew straight rows of stitches—they're designed only for embellishing.

If you already own a sewing machine but want to do more embroidery, this machine is an excellent tool for expanding your repertoire.

presser feet

A presser foot holds the fabric flat as the feed dogs or embroidery unit moves it along. There are lots of specialized feet that are perfect for fancy stitching. If you buy a special presser foot, make sure it fits on your machine—or buy a shank adaptor kit to make it fit correctly.

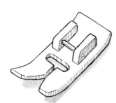

general purpose/zigzag foot: works well for most sewing purposes, with straight or zigzag stitch; underside of the foot is flat

satin stitch/appliqué/open-toe foot: features a wide groove on the bottom surface that glides over dense decorative stitches; good for appliqué, satin-stitching, cutwork, and couching

pintuck foot: forms tuck by pulling fabric through the center groove; has three, five, or seven grooves on the bottom that act as channels for the sewn tucks and spacers for subsequent tucks

cording foot: hole or guide feeds decorative trim or thread under the needle thread; if there is a groove on the bottom, it can feed more-dimensional trim, such as cording and stranded pearls

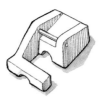

piping foot: deep groove on the bottom surface lets the machine zigzag-stitch over a string of pearls or beads

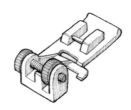

sequin and ribbon foot: feeds trim through a small tube so the machine can zigzag-stitch over the trim to hold it in place

overedge/overcast foot: forms stitches over the raw edge to prevent fraying and curling and for decorative purposes

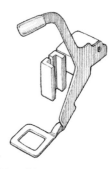

embroidery/darning foot: designed for machine darning, and free-motion embroidery; may have an attached spring to facilitate the high-speed, up-and-down movement of the needle

braiding foot: holds narrow braids or cord in place through an opening in the front as the machine zigzag-stitches over them

needles

Machine-embroidering tends to dull the sewing-machine needle, so replace the needle frequently—about every three hours of stitch time. Doing so will minimize stitching problems and will produce clean, smooth, accurate stitches. Always use the sewing-machine needles recommended by the manufacturer of your machine.

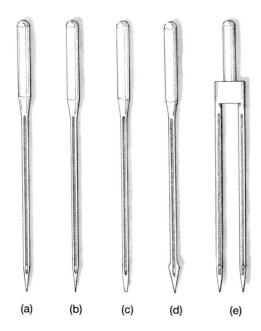

(a)   (b)   (c)   (d)   (e)

Needle Style

There are three basic needle styles: universals (a), sharps (b), and ballpoints (c). There are also many variations of them for decorative and specialty stitching, including the wedge point (d) and twin needle (e). Machine-embroidery needles (in sharp and ballpoint styles) are designed with an elongated eye and shaped scarf (or lower section) to reduce the risk of breaking the thread.

Needle Size

Needles are sized with two numbers, one for American and one for European markets, ranging from 8/60 to 19/120. Size 12/80 is ideal for most medium-weight fabrics. Smaller needles, size 11/75, are best for lightweight fabrics and designs with a lot of detail. Medium- to heavyweight fabrics require a larger needle—size 14/90 is usually a good choice.

Be sure the eye of the needle is large enough for the thread. To test, thread the loose needle and hold the thread vertically. Spin the needle. It should slide down the thread. If it doesn't, find a larger needle.

choosing the right needle

For general sewing and for decorative stitching, you'll get the best results by matching the needle to the project requirements. Consider the weave and weight of your fabric, the fiber content and thickness of your thread, and the type of stitches you'll use. Here are some guidelines.

As a general rule, select the needle style based on the type of fabric and the needle size based on the weight of the fabric. If you are working with novelty thread, choose a needle that accommodates the weight and texture of the thread.

Titanium-coated embroidery needles, which resist the adhesive in stabilizers, last five times longer than other embroidery needles.

Needle Type	Features	Best Fabric, Thread, or Use	Size
Ballpoint	Rounded point	Knit fabrics	10/70 to 16/100
Denim	Extra-sharp point	Densely woven fabrics	10/70 to 18/110
Embroidery	Elongated eye	Rayon, metallic, polyester; dense design threads	9/65 to 14/90
Metallic	Large groove minimizes shredding	Metallic threads	10/70 to 14/90
Sharp	Sharp point, slender shaft	Any weight wovens	8/60 to 14/90
Spring	Spring around needle acts like presser foot	Free-motion embroidery, monograms	11/75 to 16/100
Topstitch	Extra-large eye	Heavy topstitching threads	12/80 to 16/100
Twin or Triple	Multiple needles on a single shank	Stitches two or three parallel rows; first number indicates distance between needles	1.6 mm/70 to 4.0 mm/100
Universal	Slightly rounded point	Most knits and wovens	8/60 to 19/120

sewing and measuring tools

These basic sewing and measuring tools will make decorative stitching easy. You'll find some of them absolutely indispensable. Keep an assortment handy.

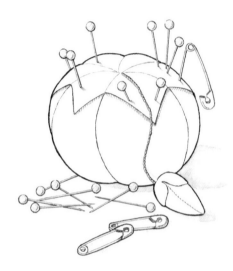

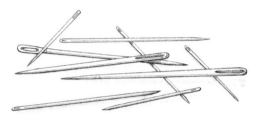

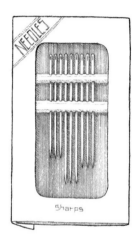

straight pins: Choose smooth, straight, and rust-free pins. A pincushion keeps them easily accessible.

hand-sewing needles: These needles come in sizes 1 to 26. The larger the number, the shorter and finer the needle. Betweens are short with round eyes, often used in quilting. Embroidery or crewel needles are medium length with large eyes to accommodate decorative thread or yarn.

seam gauge: A seam gauge is a small ruler with a sliding indicator that is used to measure small areas.

iron: Choose an iron that produces a reliable amount of steam. Work with a press cloth between the iron and the fabric to avoid damaging your project.

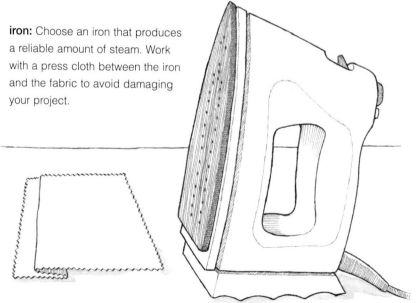

transparent ruler: A see-through ruler, 2" (5.1 cm) wide, with horizontal and vertical measurement markings, ensures precise placement of trim, appliqués, and embroidery motifs.

marking tools

Marking tools make temporary guidelines to help you position trims, decorative stitching, and hoops for motif embroidery. Test any marking tool inside the item or on scrap fabric to make sure the markings can be completely removed. To avoid leftover marks, choose the marker that most closely matches the fabric color— but be sure it is clearly visible.

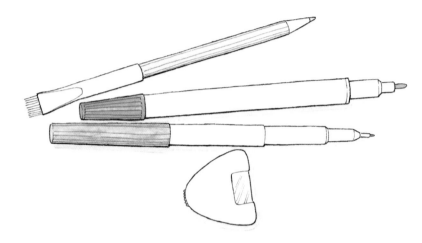

chalk wedge or pencil: Chalk is an easy way to copy design lines or placement lines. It tends to rub off, so mark the fabric just before you're ready to sew.

fabric-marking pens: The markings made by water-soluble ink pens can be removed with a damp cloth. They shouldn't be used on fabrics that are very lightweight or that are dry-clean only. Air-soluble ink disappears on its own within 48 hours. Pressing can set these marks permanently, so remove the markings before ironing.

fabric-marking pencils: These pencils contain less graphite than standard pencils, so the lines don't smudge. Markings come off with damp water or with machine washing.

If you have a very light touch, you can mark with a regular No. 2 pencil. The markings are visible for a while, but disappear with regular wash and wear.

cutting tools

Good-quality, sharp scissors are essential. Keep them separate from house-hold scissors—and never let anyone use them to cut paper. It's also a good idea to have your scissors sharpened from time to time.

seam ripper: This tiny clawlike tool enables you to remove unwanted stitches without ripping the fabric.

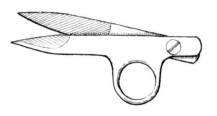

thread snips: With only one finger hole, these short, sharp blades are ideal for cutting threads.

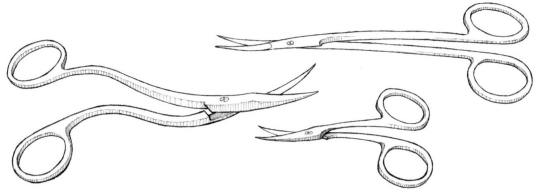

embroidery scissors: Single- and double-curved scissors are helpful when embroidering. They have a slight curve at the end of the blades so that you can get the tips under the threads that you need to trim. Double-curved models make it easier to trim threads that are in an embroidery hoop.

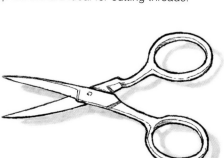

straight-tip scissors: These are small scissors—usually 3" to 4" (7.6 to 10.2 cm) long—with two sharp points for precision cutting. They're great for cutting away stabilizer and trimming seams.

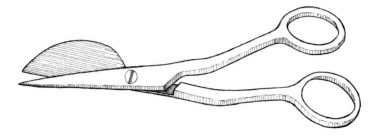

appliqué scissors: These scissors have one wide blade that lifts the fabric, so you can trim a top layer without cutting the layer underneath.

machine accessories

For convenience, safety, and efficiency, consider investing in a few extra accessories. You don't need all of them at first, but as you embroider more often, you'll find them helpful.

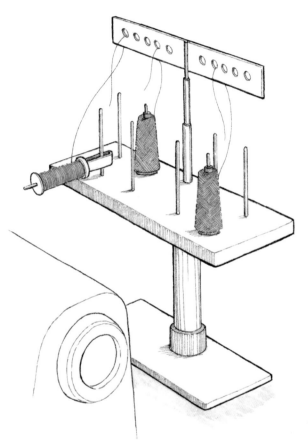

thread/spool holders: For decorative stitching, you often work with several thread colors. A multiple-spool holder holds all the spools you need—and above the machine to reduce tension on the thread.

It's ideal to have both vertical and horizontal spool pins. Parallel-wound thread feeds off the spool more easily on a vertical spool pin. Cross-wound thread feeds off the spool more consistently when the pin is horizontal.

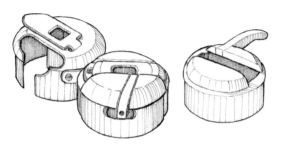

extra bobbin case: On machines with a front-loading bobbin, the bobbin is inserted into a removable bobbin case and then into the machine. The bobbin case controls the tension of the bobbin thread.

If you are working with heavy or textured threads, you might need to adjust the tension by turning the tension screw. Purchase an extra bobbin case that you can adjust for specialty threads so you can keep the original case at the factory-set tension.

surge protector: Your machine is a significant investment, so protect it just as you would your computer or any other piece of valuable equipment.

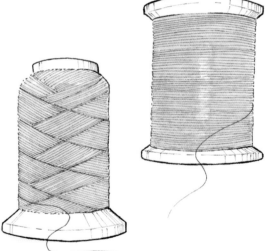

fabric selection

You can decorate any type of fabric, but some fabrics are easier to work with than others—and some showcase your creative stitches better than others. With the right combination of stitch design and stabilizer, you can embellish even the most challenging fabrics.

Fabric and Stitch Density

The best part of decorative machine stitching is that, with the right design and the right stabilizer, you can embroider on almost any fabric. It's important to consider the stitch density and to choose a design that your fabric can handle.

Stitch density is the number of stitches per square inch (or centimeter) of an area. Outline-only designs have a very low stitch density. Designs that are completely filled with stitches have a high density.

As a rule, densely stitched designs work best in medium- to heavyweight fabrics. Designs that are less dense work well with lightweight, sheer fabrics that have a smooth surface. You can minimize stitch density by embroidering with a finer thread. Or you can support the stitched area of the fabric with stabilizer.

With high-end embroidery machines and machine-embroidery editing or resizing software, you can adjust the size and density of any design.

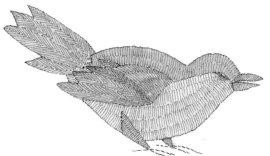

loosely woven fabrics: Open weaves of any weight are challenging. They become distorted during stitching. Stabilize them before you put them in a hoop. The stabilizer adds a second layer, which creates a more stable surface for stitching.
best design choices: open designs, designs with low stitch density and minimal stitches, or long stitches

tightly woven fabrics: Stable weaves are the easiest to embroider, especially if they have a smooth surface. They come in many weights. Popular choices include broadcloth, canvas, and chambray in linen, cotton, and polyester blends.
best design choices: all designs

heavyweight fabrics: Thick fabrics are difficult to hoop, but they're usually pretty stable, so the stitched designs look great. If the fabric is too heavy to hoop, work with the hoopless embroidery method (see page 73).

You can stitch fairly dense designs on heavy fabric, but if the stitches are too dense, the motif might cup and the fabric around it might pucker. If so, edit the stitch design (see pages 60 and 64) to eliminate some of the stitches or change to a finer thread. Be sure you have bobbin-only thread in the bobbin (see page 20).
best design choices: designs with moderate to high stitch density and open or filled patterns

nonwoven fabrics: Interfacing, felt, and synthetic suede should be hooped. Make sure the design isn't too dense, or the stitching might bunch up on the wrong side or perforate the fabric and create holes or tears.
best design choices: designs with low to moderate stitch density

sheer and lightweight fabrics: You have to stabilize these delicate fabrics so the stitches don't tear them. Opt for a piece of self-fabric as the stabilizer or select mesh stabilizer, which is translucent and won't show on the right side. If you use self-fabric, position the two pieces so the straight grains are perpendicular to each other. Trim away the excess stabilizer close to the stitching.
best design choices: open designs with low stitch density

Slippery fabrics can be difficult to embroider. Instead, stitch the motif onto a piece of organdy, organza, or netting and then sew it onto the fabric as an appliqué.

knit and pile fabrics

Don't be afraid to work with stretchy, textured, or plush fabrics. T-shirts, velvet dresses, fleece jackets, and even beach towels all look great with a little embroidery— all you need are the right stitch design and the right stabilizer (see pages 21 and 24).

stretch knit fabrics, T-shirts, and sweatshirts: Knits are unstable by nature. If the fabric stretches while you are embroidering, the stitches will distort. The fabric can be damaged by a build-up of stitches, too.

Before hooping a knit, stabilize the embroidery area with fusible tricot-knit interfacing. Add cut-away stabilizer under the area and, if necessary, a water-soluble topper (see page 24). Avoid very dense designs that make the fabric stiff.
best design choices: designs with low to moderate stitch density, low stitch count, or long stitches

napped and pile fabrics: Not all designs look good on pile fabrics—so test your design on scrap fabric. To avoid crushing the pile, don't hoop fleece, velour, or velvet and work with the hoopless technique (see page 73). Attach cut-away stabilizer under the fabric and a water-soluble stabilizer on top (if the fabric is not damaged by water).

The topping prevents the stitches from sinking into the fabric pile. If the stitches do sink, opt instead for a permanent, vinyl-topping stabilizer in a color that matches the stitching. Cut it away close to the stitching. Avoid iron-away stabilizers, which will crush the pile when you remove them.
best design choices: designs that are either very open, with outline stitches, or that are very dense

embroidery thread

Embroidery thread is specially made to withstand the stress of high-speed machine embroidery. Don't ever embroider with regular sewing thread. Embroidery thread comes in a variety of weights, textures, fibers, and colors—and each creates a different effect, depending on your stitches and your design.

Tips for Successful Embroidery

- Make a trial stitch-out (a completely stitched sample) of your design. Work with the same type of thread, fabric, stabilizer, and interfacing that you'll use on the final project.

- Adjust the sewing machine tension, as needed (see page 29). In general, loosen the top thread tension slightly to ensure even stitches. Test the stitching before beginning the project.

- Insert a new needle (see page 9) if the thread breaks or if the machine skips stitches.

- Slide a thread net over the spool if the thread is slippery.

- To be sure the thread feeds through the machine smoothly, place the notched end of a vertical thread spool down. On a horizontal spool pin, place the notched end toward the right.

- Synthetic threads are likely to stretch, so sew more slowly when working with these to avoid distorting the stitching.

- Always sew at a steady, moderate speed.

Thread Weight

The higher the number, the finer the thread. For example, 30-weight thread is thicker and heavier than 40-weight thread. The most popular machine-embroidery thread is 40-weight, and most embroidery motifs are designed for this weight of thread.

To get a better feeling for how stitches and threads work together, make a sampler of the same stitch in several different thread weights. For satin stitching and to fill an area, work with heavier thread (30 weight). Choose finer thread (40 to 60 weight) for very dense designs. Try varying thread weights within a design to create texture. Make notes and keep the sampler for future reference.

It's okay to combine different thread types and brands in a single project as long as they share the same care requirements.

thread choices

Embroidery thread is like a painter's palette, with hundreds of wonderful fibers, colors, and textures to choose from! With the right thread, your designs will lie flat and smooth and look great. Polyester and rayon threads are the most popular and easy to obtain.

cotton thread: For a matte finish and soft texture, work with cotton thread. It's great for both construction and decorative stitching, particularly on quilts and heirloom sewing. Choose cotton thread for machine stitching that simulates the look of hand-embroidery.

Cotton thread has the most weight options—from 20 weight (for couching, see page 42) to 80 weight (for very delicate stitching and dense embroidery designs). There are hundreds of color options.

Care suggestions: Can be machine-washed in cold water. Tumble-dry with moderate heat setting or hang to dry. Do not bleach.

metallic thread: These fancy threads add sparkle and shine, but need careful handling. They are most suitable for long and open stitches.

Before stitching, run the thread between your fingers to make sure it feels smooth with no jagged bits. If the thread kinks as you sew, switch the thread to a vertical spool pin (see page 13). It also helps to work with larger spools of thread. Choose the thinnest bobbin thread you can—and a metallic-specific needle. Loosen the upper thread tension and stitch slowly.

Care suggestions: Machine-wash in lukewarm or cool water with mild detergent. Tumble-dry on low heat. Press with an iron on the heat setting for synthetics.

polyester thread: For durable and colorfast stitching, polyester is an excellent choice. Polyester filament and polyester trilobal thread have nearly the same amount of luster and high sheen as rayon. (Spun polyester and cotton-covered polyester thread, with matte finishes, are mainly for garment construction.)

Polyester thread can be bleached and it won't shrink, fade, or bleed—so it's ideal for decorating children's clothing and frequently laundered items. It stretches, so tighten the machine's upper thread tension as needed.

Care suggestions: Can be machine-washed and machine-dried with hot water. Bleach as needed. Press with a cool iron.

rayon thread: Lustrous and shiny, rayon thread is available in 30, 40, or 50 weight, and in a huge variety of colors. Rayon is supple, so the embroidered stitching will be, too. Rayon thread isn't as strong as cotton thread, so don't use it for construction. Loosen the machine's upper thread tension slightly, if necessary, to ensure smooth stitches.

Care suggestions: Can be machine-washed and machine-dried in warm water with mild soap or detergent. Do not use chlorine bleach. Press with a warm iron if needed.

special-effects threads: Novelty threads can do amazing things. *Variegated thread* creates the illusion of shading and texture. *Silk thread* is strong and luxurious, but expensive—so save it for special projects. *Monofilament nylon* in a clear or smoky color is almost invisible when stitched. Flat, lightweight *ribbon threads* create great surface effects, but can be loaded in bobbins only (see page 39). *Ultraviolet-activated thread* changes color in sunlight. *Glow-in-the dark thread* is great for pajamas, costumes, and active sportswear worn outdoors after dark.

Topstitching thread creates highly visible decorative stitches. For *wooly nylon* and *wooly acrylic,* you need to work with a large-eyed sewing-machine needle or a serger. *Serger threads* are available in the same fibers as embroidery threads. Novelty and *heavyweight serger threads* are threaded in the bottom loopers.

Care suggestions: Varies. Check manufacturer's recommendation.

Thread lubricants will reduce friction and fraying — but you can't use them with all machines, so be sure to check your owner's manual first.

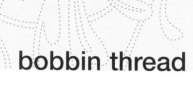

bobbin thread

The bobbin thread is just as important as the decorative thread. You can thread the bobbin and needle with the same thread—but it's better to work with a thread specifically designed for the bobbin. You'll save money, too. If you aren't going to see the wrong side of the project, save the more-expensive specialty threads for the right side!

bobbin thread: This special thread is very fine, so it reduces bulk in an embroidered design by reducing the amount of thread on the wrong side of the fabric. It also helps keep dense designs flexible and flat. A popular choice is 60-weight cotton bobbin thread, which is strong but also soft next to the skin. Polyester and nylon bobbin thread in the same weight are also strong, but not as comfortable.

Before you start embroidering, fill several bobbins in black, white, or a color that matches the upper thread, so you don't have to wind a new bobbin in the middle of stitching a design. Always make a new bobbin by starting with an empty bobbin and run the machine at half-speed so the thread winds evenly and without stretching.

prewound bobbins: You can buy prewound bobbins. They are a great time saver and usually hold more thread than the standard bobbin. They can be generic or specific to the machine brand. Before purchasing the generic type, make sure your machine accepts them.

Prewound bobbins with black or white thread are easiest to find, but more colors are becoming available, especially in cotton thread. If your machine has a low bobbin indicator, you have to remove the cardboard on the sides of the bobbins so the sensor can operate properly.

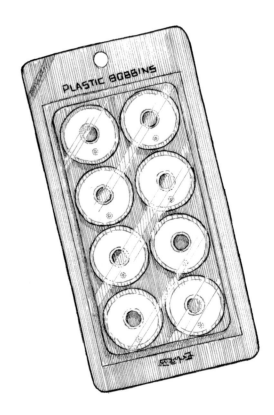

Cotton thread produces more lint than polyester or rayon. Clean the bobbin area frequently with a small brush or pipe cleaner.

about stabilizers

Stabilizers are essential to professional-looking machine embroidery. These materials, whether woven or nonwoven, support the project fabric during stitching. They also prevent fabric from slipping or stretching in hoops or while stitching. Stabilizers minimize puckers, tunneling, and distortion in the stitched design.

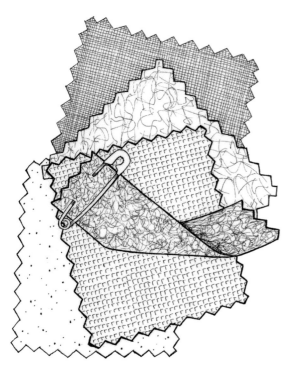

Tips for Working with Stabilizers

Stabilizers are easy to work with. Simply affix a piece of stabilizer to the wrong side of the fabric, behind the embroidery area. Stitch through both layers. When you've finished stitching, remove the excess stabilizer. Here are some tips for getting the best results:

- Match the weights of the fabric and stabilizer. If the stabilizer is too heavy, the embroidery will be stiff. If it's too light, the embroidery might buckle.
- Choose a dark-colored stabilizer for dark fabrics and light-colored or white stabilizer for light-colored fabrics. The stabilizer should not change the color of the fabric.
- For light-colored and lightweight fabrics, you can also choose mesh stabilizer. It will be transparent from the right side of the fabric.
- Dense designs and unstable fabrics require a heavy stabilizer.
- For fabric that stretches, choose cut-away stabilizer (see page 23).
- For stretchy or unstable fabrics, you can also work with an adhesive or fusible stabilizer (see page 25).
- Double or triple the layers of stabilizer if the fabric needs extra support.
- Never apply cut-away stabilizer to the right side of the fabric. Some of this permanent stabilizer will remain under the stitches and will be visible around the edges of your embroidery.
- To adhere fusible stabilizers (see page 25), set your iron to dry (without steam).
- Practice stitching on stabilized fabric scraps before embroidering on your project.
- Trim the excess stabilizer with utility scissors. It can dull your good fabric scissors.
- Trim multiple stabilizers separately and to different widths to avoid a bulky edge.

types of stabilizers

Stabilizers are applied in several ways—by basting, fusing, or with spray adhesive—but they are categorized by how you remove them once they've done their job. There are four main types of stabilizers: cut-away, tear-away, water-soluble, and iron-away. Sometimes you need to combine them to get the best results.

Every stabilizer comes in a variety of weights. All stabilizers, except for iron-away types, can be purchased with an adhesive backing (see page 25). It's a good idea to keep a file with the name of the stabilizer and comments about its performance. For more detailed information, refer to the chart on page 104.

Backing or Topping?

"Backing" and "topping" describe how particular types of stabilizer are used. Backing refers to stabilizer that is used on the wrong side of fabric under decorative stitching. You'll need backing for every machine-embroidery project.

Topping (or topper) is used on the right side of napped or pile fabrics. Topping holds down surface fibers so the decorative stitches don't sink into the fibers and vanish.

Topping comes in two varieties: A water-soluble or a tear-away, plasticlike material. Water-soluble topping, as shown in the drawing at top left, looks like a transparent film and dissolves completely in water. Tear-away topping, as shown in the drawing at bottom left, is available in an array of colors, so you can match the thread color. It also comes in a clear form, so that after the topper is torn away, the remaining bits are hardly visible.

If you have the right stabilizer, your stitches will be smooth, the design perfectly aligned, and the fabric firm and pucker-free.

Cut-away Stabilizers

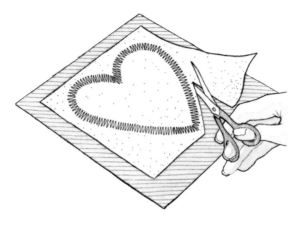

Cut-away stabilizers provide the strongest, most permanent support. They provide continued support for the fabric and the embroidery design during regular wearing and washing.

Cut-aways remain under the decorative stitching on the wrong side of the fabric. Trim the excess to within 1/4" (6 mm) of the decorative stitches (appliqué scissors are helpful for this task). Round the corners, to minimize the amount of show-through on the right side. Apply cut-away stabilizers to knits, stretch wovens, denim, leather and suede, and open-weave fabrics.

Tear-away Stabilizers

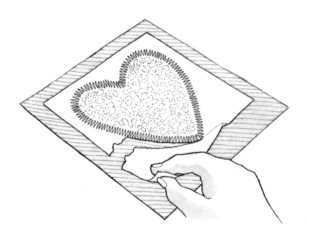

Tear-aways provide good support for dense stitch designs. They are applied to the wrong side of the fabric. They support the fabric while you stitch, and visible excess is torn away after the stitching is complete. If there are small traces left when you tear it away, remove them with tweezers. Or just wait—they'll come out in the wash.

Tear-aways are best on stable, woven fabrics, such as quilting fabrics, polyester–cotton blends, and most nonstretch fabrics. As you stitch, the needle perforates the stabilizer. These perforations make it easy to tear off the stabilizer later. It's easier to remove if the stitches are close together. Pull carefully, keeping the stabilizer as flat to the fabric as you can. Take care not to stretch the fabric or distort the stitches. If the stabilizer doesn't give way easily, cut it instead with sharp embroidery scissors. Test several brands to find one that tears easily in every direction.

For extra support, apply two or three layers of lightweight tear-away stabilizer. Gently remove each layer individually.

Water-soluble Stabilizers

Water-soluble stabilizers dissolve when they come in contact with moisture. They are available as plastic sheets, lightweight paper, spray, and liquid. These stabilizers are good as toppers because they can be completely removed after stitching. If your fabric is washable, they're great for delicate and loose-weave fabrics and open embroidery designs.

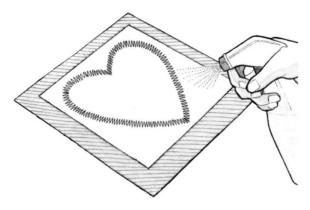

- Paper-thin sheets of water-soluble stabilizer make good backings or toppers. To remove them, either soak the project in water or apply a fine mist of water with a spray bottle, according to the manufacturer's instructions. Store these products in an airtight plastic bag so they don't dry out or become sticky from humidity.

- Spray-on stabilizer is similar to starch. Generously spray one side of the fabric with the stabilizer and press the fabric on the other side to stiffen it. You still need a second stabilizer for your stitching. Tear-away is a good option in most cases.

- Liquid stabilizer stiffens when you brush it on the fabric. Let it dry completely before you stitch. The fabric will be easier to hoop. You'll need to apply a second type of stabilizer on the wrong side of the fabric.

Iron-away Stabilizers

Iron-away stabilizers are ideal for fabric that is nonwashable, delicate, or sheer. The fabric must be able to tolerate high iron temperatures. There are two kinds of iron-aways: woven and plastic.

Woven iron-away stabilizer turns into brown flakes when you heat it with a dry iron. After stitching, trim away as much excess as you can. Heat the remaining stabilizer with the iron, working with a press cloth. Brush away the flakes.

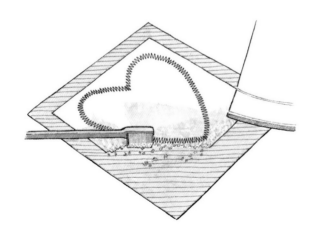

Plastic sheets of stabilizer are used as toppers. The topper remains under the stitching as extra support. Cut away the excess and then lightly touch the surface of the stabilizer with a hot, dry iron. The stabilizer turns into little beads that you can just wipe away with a paper towel.

Brush away the flaky residue of iron-aways with a new toothbrush or other small, clean, rigid brush.

securing stabilizers

There are many ways to apply stabilizers to your fabric. Often, you can simply baste the stabilizer and fabric together by hand or machine. For stable, nonslippery fabrics (especially medium- to heavyweight ones), you can just hoop the two layers together (see page 72). When you need extra security—for example, with slippery or unstable fabrics—you can work with special adhesive products. Here are some of the many choices:

iron-on or fusible stabilizers: Heat activates the temporary adhesive coating on one surface of these stabilizers. Iron-ons and fusibles are great for slippery, bias-cut, and unstable fabrics, because they keep the fabric from stretching during hooping and stitching. After stitching, gently separate the excess stabilizer from the fabric and either trim it or tear it away.

self-adhesive stabilizers: These products have an adhesive coating on one side that is protected by a waxlike removable paper. They are ideal for both hooped and hoopless embroidery (see page 73). Simply peel off the protective sheet and lay the fabric or project on the adhesive surface, smoothing it carefully.

water-activated adhesive stabilizers: Moisten the adhesive side with a damp sponge, then lay the fabric (right side up) on top, and smooth away any wrinkles. You can reposition the stabilizer by remoistening the edges. After stitching, remoisten the edges so you can gently lift the stabilizer and trim away the excess. This type works well for both hooped and hoopless stitching.

spray adhesives: Spray glues are helpful when you are working with a nonadhesive stabilizer. Just spray the temporary adhesive onto the stabilizer. Be sure to work in a room with good ventilation. You can affix the stabilizer to the fabric before hooping or hoop the stabilizer first and then adhere the fabric. Never spray the project or the embroidery machine. Do not combine spray adhesives with water-soluble or iron-away stabilizers.

Remove adhesive residue from the fabric and hoop as soon as possible, before it sets. You can buy special products for removing residue or you can wipe the hoop with Lectric Shave—it works!

prepare your work space

Organize your sewing space and equipment so you are ready to stitch whenever you get the urge. If you're lucky, you have a sewing space where you can leave your machines and supplies set up all the time. Most people sew on their kitchen or dining room tables—which is okay, too. Here are some hints for making the most of it.

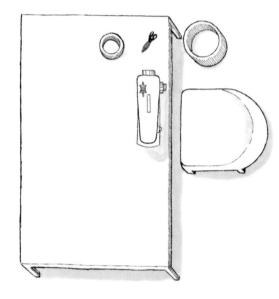

Tools and Materials

Commandeer a shelf in a closet and keep all your supplies and machines together. It's important that you can see everything—so keep thread, notions, and tools in clear-plastic, labeled boxes. Keep design memory cards and disks in a three-ring binder with plastic sleeves and label them. Store each type of stabilizer in its own labeled plastic bag.

Your Sewing Area

Your sewing table should be large enough to fit your machines, fabric, and, if possible, a thread rack to keep your embroidery threads organized. Keep the area around the machine clear. The movement of the embroidery hoop could knock over notions (or your coffee cup!).

You'll also need a comfortable chair, a wastebasket, and adequate lighting. An extra gooseneck lamp directs task lighting right where you need it. Set up an ironing board nearby.

If your machine vibrates when in use, spread a sheet of rubber shelf liner on your sewing table to keep it in place.

prepare your machine

For the best sewing experience, know your machine. Check your owner's manual for bobbin and threading instructions and suggestions for routine maintenance. Attach or activate the embroidery unit, if you have one. Before you begin, take a few minutes to gather all your supplies. If you are organized ahead of time, you'll be able to focus on having fun at the machine.

- Have several bobbins wound and ready. Load a full bobbin into the machine.

- Insert a new needle after sewing for more than eight hours or embroidering for more than three.

- Brush the bobbin area and the area under the needle to remove lint. Most machines come with a small lint brush.

- Thread your machine correctly. Follow the marked thread path or refer to your owner's manual. If your stitch quality is unsatisfactory, rethread. Nine times out of ten, stitch problems are the result of improper threading.

- Draw the bobbin thread to the top before starting to stitch. (On some machines, this step is not necessary, so check your manual.) Hold the needle thread and turn the balance wheel toward you one full rotation. As the needle drops, the top thread interlocks with the bobbin thread and brings it up through the needle hole. Pull both threads together under the presser foot and off to the side or back.

- Move your needle to its highest position. Hold both threads toward the back as you begin to sew to prevent the threads from tangling or jamming on the first few stitches.

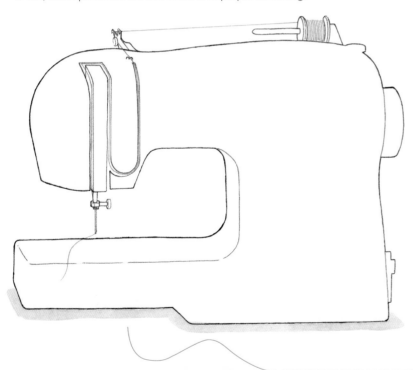

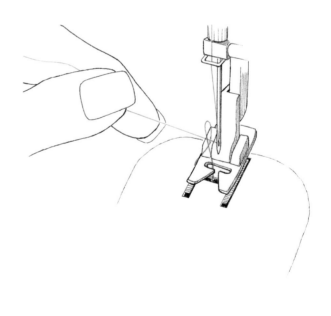

prepare
your fabric

Whether you plan to embellish fabric yardage or a ready-made item (called a blank), take the time to prepare the fabric before stitching. These preliminary steps will improve the quality of your stitching and finished embroidery.

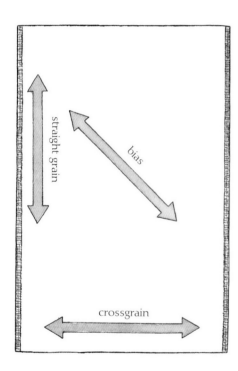

- Start with good-quality fabric. A quality fabric will last longer and is less likely to stretch or distort during stitching.
- Make sure the stabilizer that you select has the same care requirements as the fabric or item (see page 22).
- Preshrink everything.
- Press the fabric or blank to remove all wrinkles. They'll distort your decorative stitching.
- If your fabric looks the same on both sides, mark the right side of the fabric (see page 11).
- Check the grain of the fabric. Fabric grain refers to the direction of the woven threads. Position the stitching to run along the lengthwise grain (parallel to the finished edge) or crosswise grain (perpendicular to the finished edge). Avoid sewing long rows of stitching on the bias grain (diagonal between lengthwise and crosswise grains). Bias grain is very stretchy and distorts easily.

Preshrinking Fabric

You do not want your fabric to shrink after you've stitched it—so wash it ahead of time. Washing removes starch or sizing, which might deflect the needle. Toss any machine-washable items in the washer and dryer before stitching.

For dry-clean-only items, either steam the fabric to preshrink it or have it dry-cleaned. To preshrink with steam, start by steam-pressing a small scrap or inside area to make sure the steam doesn't harm the fabric. If the fabric passes the test, dampen a press cloth and press the wrong side of the fabric until the water has evaporated. Shoot steam into the fibers as you press.

about stitch tension

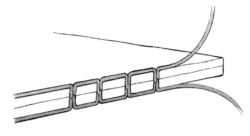

correct tension for sewing

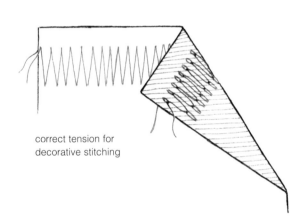

correct tension for
decorative stitching

Correct thread tension is the key to a perfectly balanced stitch. Check your machine manual for tension adjustment instructions. Some machines adjust tension automatically.

Thread Tension for Sewing

When you're sewing seams, the top and bobbin threads should interlock midway between the fabric layers. To check that your stitch tension is balanced, sew a seam with different-colored needle and bobbin threads. If both thread colors are visible on the top of the fabric, loosen the upper thread tension. If you can see both threads on the back, tighten it.

Thread Tension for Decorative Stitching

For most decorative stitching, you want a slightly unbalanced tension, so that the top thread is pulled slightly to the wrong side. None of the bobbin thread should be visible on the right side. If it is, loosen the top thread tension. The bobbin tension is factory set, so you shouldn't change it (see page 39).

Most computerized embroidery machines adjust the top thread tension automatically. If you need to adjust the upper thread tension manually, make a very small adjustment, as your machine manual suggests. Then test the results until the tension is right.

The best way to check your thread tension is to stitch a column of zigzag stitches on a scrap of fabric that has been stabilized (see pages 21–25). On the wrong side of the fabric, you should see the bobbin thread only in the center third of the column of stitches. The top thread should show on the outside thirds.

check before you stitch

Ready, set, stitch! Follow this checklist of steps before you sit down at the machine, and you'll sail through your project—and love the results!

✓ Organize your sewing area. Position the sewing machine on the right side of your work table, so the bulk of the fabric rests on the left side. Keep a wastebasket nearby or tape a small trash bag to the edge of the worktable to catch thread snips and fabric scraps.

✓ Throughout your work area, provide adequate overhead lighting and task lighting for close-up work.

✓ Set up an iron and ironing board. Keep a press cloth handy, too (a scrap of muslin works well).

✓ Gather all the sewing tools and notions you need. Keep sewing scissors, pins, a pincushion, and a seam ripper within easy reach.

✓ Prepare and preshrink your fabric or blank. Press out all creases and wrinkles.

✓ If you have many thread colors in your design, organize your spools.

✓ After embroidering for more than three hours, insert a new needle in the machine.

✓ Fill several bobbins with bobbin thread (see page 20) or with the same thread that you're working with on the thread spool.

✓ Brush the bobbin area, feed dogs, and tension disks with a small brush to remove lint.

✓ Stabilize a scrap of fabric so you can practice your stitches. Notice the length and tension of the stitches and make any necessary adjustments.

✓ Take a deep breath, relax, and begin—and, most important, have fun!

sources for design ideas

Every sewer has his or her own design aesthetic. That's what makes fabric embellishment so exciting. With a little practice, your designs will express your individual style perfectly.

If you are intimidated by the thought of creating something from nothing, remember, inspiration is all around you. Mother Nature is an endless source, so take a walk through the park or along the beach and wait for inspiration to strike.

Illustrated magazines, books, and catalogs also provide countless ideas. Look at the patterned clothing, linens, toys, pillows, and home décor in a department store. Make notes and draw sketches of those details or patterns that catch your eye.

Rummage through your stash for fabrics, trims, buttons, beads, and ribbons that you love. Keep a file of paint chips, china patterns, magazine pages, greeting cards, wrapping paper, fabric and trim swatches, and anything else you find appealing. You'll be surprised to see how often you're attracted to the same colors and shapes.

When you're ready to start designing, pull out your sketches and scraps—and your copy of *Singer Simple Decorative Machine Stitching*. There's no right or wrong in creative design. Experiment with ideas and materials—and then just see what happens!

embroidery designs

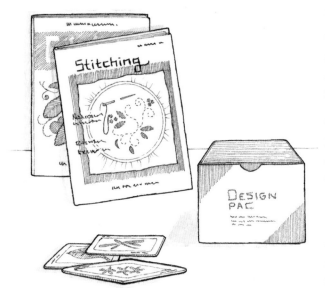

Whether you choose to design your own embroidery or customize a premade design (of which there are thousands!), you make any design unique with your choice of color, thread, and stitches.

Working with Existing Designs

The simplest way to start is with premade embroidery designs (also called stock designs). Sewing-machine manufacturers and independent design companies sell designs for computerized embroidery machines—and some offer them for free! Hand-embroidery designs are easy to find too.

You can customize any type of premade embroidery design. Simply change the thread colors, move sections within the design, and add or eliminate stitches (see pages 60–64). Other important factors that affect the end result are your choice of the background fabric and the placement of the design.

Elements of Design

When you're designing a motif, consider the following components. Make preliminary color sketches to create your palette. Think about the composition and where you want to place the motif on the garment or fabric.

color: the hues and tones that occur and repeat throughout the embroidery design

composition: the overall shapes, lines, and layout of the embellishment

placement: the specific location and orientation of the design on the fabric or blank

stitch variety: the individual stitches that create pattern and texture in your design

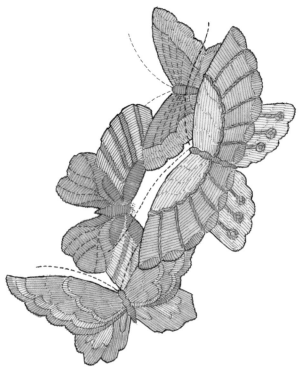

creating original designs

A successful embroidery design complements and enhances the entire project. How do you create a good design? It's easier than you think!

Drawing a Design

Start with any motif or image that pleases your eye. Study the overall shape and the individual elements, too. Trace a single element or a section of the design. Draw several variations—eliminating lines, simplifying shapes, or changing proportions. You can also rearrange, delete, or repeat elements. Don't copy—instead, try to interpret the elements in your own style.

Make several tracings and pick the one you like best. Reduce or enlarge the final design on a photocopy machine if you want to change the size. Once you have the outline and shape you like, you're ready to think about color and stitch patterns.

Designing a Motif

These four principles of design will help you create an original motif—or adapt an existing one. Keep these tips in mind as you sketch, refining your drawings as you work through the process.

- Create a *focal point,* a part of the design that attracts the eye. If the design consists of repeated patterns, each repeat should have its own focal point.
- Strive for *harmony* within the design. Don't let a single section of the design detract from the rest.
- Maintain *proportion.* The motifs and stitches should complement each other. Keep their sizes relative to each other, so no one part dominates and throws off the overall design.
- Strive for *balance* within the design itself. Symmetry around a central point is pleasing to the eye.

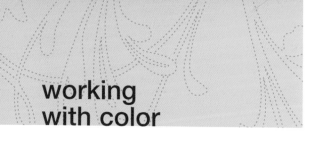

working with color

The right colors can turn an okay design into a fabulous one. When you're choosing thread colors, consider the color of the background fabric, the type of design you're stitching, and the colors you like best.

Working with the Color Wheel

A color wheel contains all the primary and secondary colors. It's a great place to start when you are planning colors. There are three basic color schemes that will almost always guarantee a beautiful design.

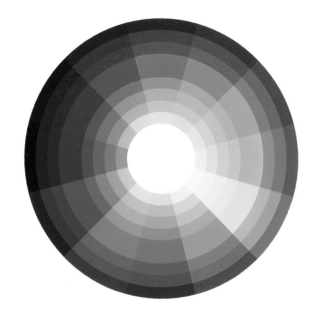

Monochromatic colors are different values or shades of the same color. A range of shades of a single color creates a sophisticated and subtle effect.

Analogous colors are neighbors on the color wheel—for example, green, blue, and violet. Together, they look harmonious.

Complementary colors, sometimes called contrasting colors, are opposite each other on the color wheel. Pairing these colors—red and green, yellow and purple, blue and orange—will add energy and an extra punch to any design.

- A contrasting or complementary color makes a great accent in any color scheme.
- Brighten any color by placing it next to its color complement.
- Choose warm colors, such as red, yellow, and orange, when you want an image or element to "pop."
- Choose cool colors, such as blue, green, and violet, when you want an image or element to recede.
- If you are working with a patterned background fabric, choose stitch designs and motifs in colors that are harmonious with the colors of the fabric pattern.
- High-contrast color combinations are vibrant, but can be overwhelming—so don't overdo it. Position them carefully in the design. Low-contrast color combinations are elegant, but can benefit from a lively color accent.

positioning

Location, location, location! It's important in embroidery, too. Before you finalize the design, decide where you want to place it on the fabric or project. The position will help you determine the right size and proportion of your motif.

You can add decorative stitching to everything from clothes and accessories to sporting gear. Sketch a rough outline of the design or stitch a sample of it. Then pin it on the item you want to embroider to make sure you like the way it looks. Here are a few suggestions:

- on collars, cuffs, front plackets, front pockets, yokes of shirts, jackets, and vests
- on turtleneck collars
- at the center or at the hem of bath towels
- on pillowcases, sheets, and blankets
- at the center or brim of baseball caps and hats
- as an accent on belts and scarves
- on the yoke, hem, or surface of lingerie

- within quilt squares
- on side seams, pockets, and hems of pants
- on the flap or surface of purses and bags
- on sports clothing or gear
- on the fronts, pockets, or ties of aprons
- on soft toys
- on placemats, tablecloths, and dish towels

Guidelines for Shirt Fronts

T-shirts are one of the most popular garments to embroider. Here are some suggestions for design placements.

- Left chest: 7" to 9" (17.8 to 22.9 cm) down from the left shoulder and 4" to 5" (10.2 to 12.7 cm) from the center front.
- Centered on chest: 3" to 4" (7.6 to 10.2 cm) down from the center front of the neck edge.

Make sure the size of your design will fit a hoop size that your machine can handle.

stitch samplers

Individual stitches are the building blocks of embroidery. A stitch sampler is a handy tool for knowing what stitches look like and how best to combine them. Consider the characteristics of each stitch: Is it flat or raised, short or long, straight or wavy, dense or sparse? Each creates its own effect in your finished design.

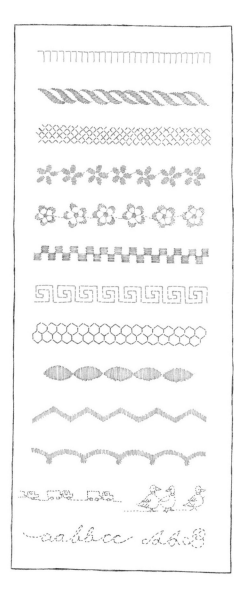

You can create wonderful effects by varying your machine's built-in basic and novelty stitches. Even the most basic machines have between 8 and 10 built-in stitches—and computerized machines often have more than 100! Most built-in stitches can be adjusted in length, width, and density. On some machines, you can rotate and mirror the stitches for even more design options (see page 38).

Make a sampler containing each stitch, experimenting by changing the width, length, or both. Mark the machine settings next to the sampler stitches with a permanent pen. You should also sew the lettering stitches (alphabets), if your machine has them, and play with their size and density. The sampler in the drawing shows some of the most popular machine stitches.

There's no need to make a sampler of digitized designs for embroidery machines. The information that comes with the design will illustrate each stitch style clearly. It is very important to stitch a test sample before you start the project.

Create custom trim or labels by sewing decorative stitches or lettering on a length of ribbon.

embroidering with a sewing machine

You'll be amazed at what you and your sewing machine can do. Your sewing machine's linear stitches can create stunning decorative stitching. From simple rows of decorative stitches to quilting and heirloom techniques—hemstitching and pintucks—your sewing machine can do just about anything you want.

Ensure that your lines of stitching are straight by drawing a placement line with a fabric-marking pen. Be sure to stabilize the fabric before you begin. Select the stitch pattern and choose your width and length settings. Stitch on the marked line, and then remove the excess stabilizer.

topstitch: Work a simple straight stitch along a seam or finished edge for a crisp, professional-looking edge. Heavier thread will make the stitching stand out. Metallic thread looks great, too.

scalloped-edge stitch: Sew this stitch along an edge. Apply seam sealant to the wrong side on the bobbin threads and on the fabric that will be trimmed away. When the seam sealant is dry, trim the fabric close to the stitching.

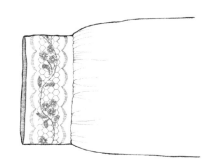

combined stitches: Overlap, overlay, and double up on decorative stitches to create your own unique pattern. Experiment on scrap fabric first. You might choose open stitches as a background, for example, with denser stitches on top for texture and edging stitches as a border.

If you have chosen a narrow, open, decorative stitch, you may not need to stabilize the fabric before stitching.

computerized sewing machines

Computerized sewing-only machines offer a variety of stitch-editing functions, such as mirror-imaging, repeating, and designing your own linear decorative stitches. Refer to your owner's manual for specifics. You might find out your machine can do a lot more than you thought.

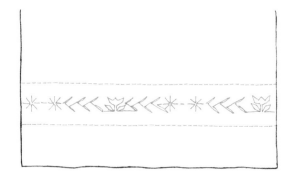

stitch length and width adjustments: These basic stitch adjustments are possible on all machines. One or both adjustments will change the appearance of decorative stitches. Make a sampler to see just how much you can vary your built-in stitches.

mirror imaging: This function doubles your stitching options—literally! It allows you to stitch mirror images of a design, horizontally and/or vertically, to create symmetrical designs. It's perfect for stitching a directional motif on each side of a collar or on either side of a monogram. You'll find this function on combination sewing/embroidery machines, too.

custom stitch sequences: On some machines, you can create your own linear stitch design by linking parts of several linear stitches into a repeating chain. If the machine includes alphabets, you can join letters to spell words.

Check your design in a mirror before you make a mirror image. Some images look off balance when reversed. Avoid mirroring designs with lettering!

bobbin work

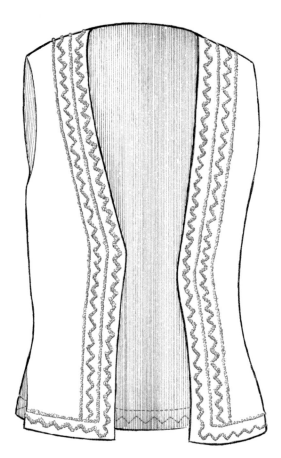

Heavy and textured threads make beautiful embroidery, but they are sometimes too thick to fit through the eye of the needle. Wind the decorative threads onto the bobbin and stitch with the fabric wrong side up. This technique, called bobbin work, lays the fancy thread on the right side of the fabric.

Suitable Threads

Novelty thread and narrow ribbon, including perle cotton, crochet thread, silk ribbon, and baby-weight yarn, are suitable choices. Wind the thread onto the bobbin by hand. Because the specialty thread is thicker than standard thread, the bobbin runs out quickly, so make several bobbins. Select all-purpose sewing thread or 30- or 40-weight rayon embroidery thread for the upper thread.

Thread Tension

If your machine has a removable bobbin case, consider buying a second bobbin case (see page 13). Reduce the bobbin-thread tension by adjusting the tension screw on the bobbin case (for front- or side-loading bobbins) or by skipping the tension slot (for top-loading bobbins).

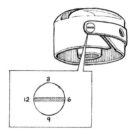

Stitching

Stabilize the wrong side of the fabric and draw the design directly on the stabilizer (the mirror image will stitch out on the right side). Hoop the fabric, if desired, with the stabilizer side up.

Make a test sample to check the tension. Look for smooth stitching on the wrong side of the fabric. The bobbin thread can be quite flat or raised and textured—whatever suits your taste.

Sew on the marked design line. The bobbin thread will stitch out underneath. When stitching is complete, pull the thread ends to the wrong side and either knot them or fuse them flat with a small piece of fusible interfacing.

free-motion embroidery

Free-motion embroidery is also called thread-painting. You can work with a standard embroidery hoop on any type of machine. When you are free-motion embroidering, you are drawing with the needle and thread. All you need is a straight or zigzag stitch. You physically move the hoop under the needle, so you can embroider shapes, random stitches, or thread-paint a landscape or picture.

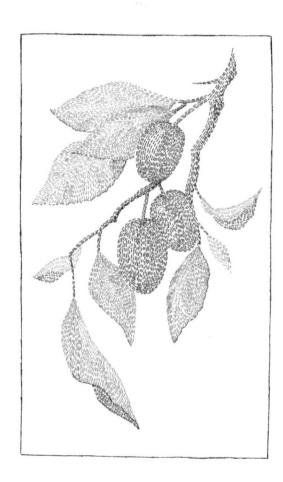

1 Stabilize the fabric. Place it in an embroidery hoop that you can slide under the needle. The wrong side of the fabric must be at the bottom of the hoop, resting on the machine bed. Make sure the fabric is in the hoop as tightly as possible.

2 Lower or cover the machine feed dogs (refer to your manual). The feed dogs are the parallel metal tracks that come up through the throat plate under the presser foot. Their job is to move the fabric, so you need to disengage them. (You can also cover the feed dogs with masking tape, but you will have to replace the tape frequently because it frays.)

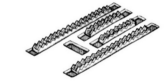

3 Install a darning presser foot or an open-toed embroidery foot—or work without a presser foot. Reduce the presser foot pressure so you can move the fabric easily.

4 Thread the machine with cotton or rayon embroidery thread. Fill the bobbin with bobbin thread. Set the stitch length and width to 0. You determine the length of the stitches by how you move the hoop. If you are stitching with zigzag stitches, set the stitch width to 2 or select the width you prefer.

5 Bring the bobbin thread to the right side so it doesn't tangle as you begin stitching. Hold both thread tails and take two or three stitches over the thread tails to secure them. Cut the thread tails.

Free-Motion Effects

Hold the edges of the hoop and move it around smoothly as the needle stitches. A side-to-side motion works best, because it's easier to see what you are stitching.

Keep the sewing machine speed moderately fast, but move the hoop slowly. If the bobbin thread shows on the right side, decrease the upper thread tension.

Experiment with different loop movements to create a range of textural and linear effects, such as:

- random motions for fill stitches
- circular movements for floral motifs
- up-and-down or side-to-side motion for grassy textures
- radial movements from a central point to create star shapes

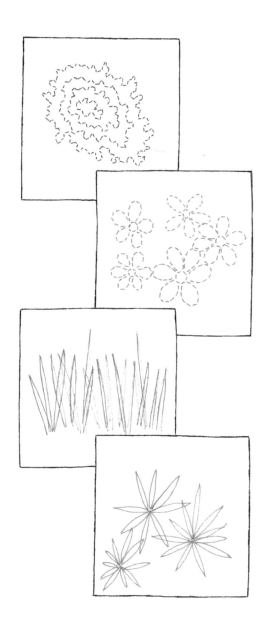

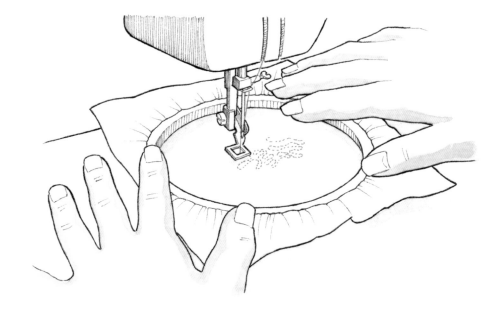

couching

Couching is a great way to embellish with narrow trim, heavy thread, yarn, ribbon, cording, or other materials that don't fit through the eye of a needle. It's also good for metallic threads that might be damaged when stitched through the fabric. When couching, you stitch trim or cord to—but not through—the surface of the fabric. Lay the couching material on the right side of the fabric. Stitch across or through the couching material to secure it.

Preparation

Attach tear-away stabilizer to the wrong side of the fabric (see page 23). Install a cording foot. Set the stitch width to the width of the trim or slightly wider.

Shorten the stitch length so you can stitch around tight curves. If the design features tight curves or corners, choose a couching material that is flexible and easily shaped.

For greater control while stitching, lower the feed dogs, insert the fabric in an embroidery hoop, and move the fabric with your hands, as in free-motion embroidery (see page 40).

Stitches

Choose a stitch that travels back and forth over the couching material, so it will secure the material to the fabric and keep the edges flat. In most cases, you can set your machine for a long decorative stitch with zigzag movement. Test the stitch on scrap fabric first to make sure it's wide enough to cover the couching material.

To adapt an open-toe presser foot for couching, wrap a piece of cellophane tape over the top of it. Puncture the center of the tape to create a hole equal to the width of the trim and the stitch.

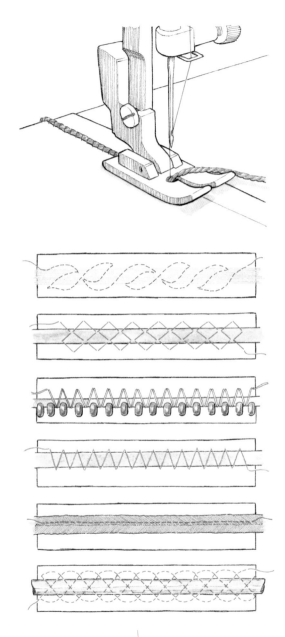

How to Couch

1. Mark a placement line on the right side of the fabric with a fabric-marking pen.

2. Hand-baste or pin tear-away stabilizer to the wrong side of the fabric.

3. Insert the decorative material (yarn, beads, cording, or other) through the opening in the front of a cording presser foot (see page 7), from front to back. If you have adapted an open-toe presser foot (see page 7), insert the material through the hole in the tape. If you are working with multiple threads, tie the ends together so they feed smoothly. Install the presser foot.

4. Thread the machine and needle with embroidery or sewing thread. Wind a bobbin with bobbin thread or other lightweight thread. Insert the bobbin.

5. Select a stitch and adjust the width so the machine stitches on either side of the couching material. Stitch slowly. As you guide the fabric, the decorative trim will feed through the presser foot.

6. Remove the stabilizer and finish the ends of the trim. To finish, either catch the ends in a seam or use a large-eye needle to pull the ends through the fabric to the wrong side. On the wrong side, either knot them, seal them with liquid fray preventer, or fuse a small patch of interfacing over the ends to hold them in place.

Tips

- Zigzag-stitch with invisible monofilament thread over strands of beads or sequins.
- Stitch a decorative stitch with contrasting thread over cording, narrow ribbon, or a cluster or thin cords.
- Straight-stitch through flat braid, such as soutache.
- Lay several threads together and feather-stitch over them with invisible thread to create a heavier line.

ribbon embroidery

Ribbon embroidery is traditionally done by hand, but you can also create it by machine. Simply machine-tack the ribbons to the fabric surface and fold or wrap them to create a design.

Silk is the ribbon of choice. It's supple and luxurious—but it's also expensive. The quality of polyester ribbon has improved so much that it is now a suitable alternative to pricey silk. Standard widths are 1/8", 1/4", 3/8", and 1/2" (2 mm, 4 mm, 7 mm, and 1.3 cm).

Before stitching, press the ribbon to remove creases. Work with fine thread in the needle. Stabilize the fabric first.

Stitching a Ribbon Bow

This easy design is a great way to try ribbon embroidery by machine. Set the machine for free-motion embroidery by lowering the feed dog. Remove the presser foot and shank. Mark the outline for the bow on the right side of the fabric with a fabric-marking pen. Mark spots for French knots. Hoop the fabric.

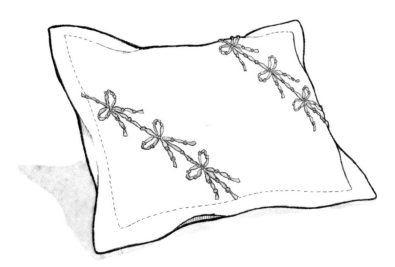

1 Cut a length of ribbon twice the overall length of the design line you want to cover. Extend the end of the ribbon 1/4" (6 mm) beyond the starting point and tack it down with two or three tiny machine stitches. Lift the ribbon and sew along the design line to the first knot mark. Extend the ribbon along the line and tack it in place on the mark.

2 With the needle down, loosely wrap the ribbon around the needle three to five times. Take one stitch so the needle moves out of the wrapped ribbon and enters the fabric slightly to the right. Stitch again over the previous stitch. You've just made a French knot.

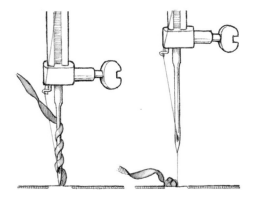

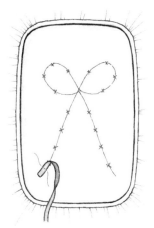

3 Repeat to the end of the marked design. Cut the ribbon end so it is the same length as the beginning strand.

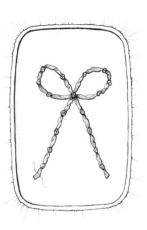

trapunto

Trapunto, often found on quilts, home décor, and garments, is a padded, decorative design. You simply stitch a design with water-soluble thread on the right side of the fabric through one or more layers of cotton or polyester batting.

Getting Started

Lower the machine feed dogs and install a darning foot. Thread an 11/75 needle or embroidery needle with water-soluble thread. Fill the bobbin with a light-weight, neutral-colored thread. You'll also need embroidery thread and quilt batting.

Stitching a Trapunto Design

1   Transfer the design to the right side of the fab-ric. Pin or baste a single or double layer of bat-ting to the wrong side of the fabric, behind the design area.

2   Place the batting and fabric under the darning foot with the right side up. Bring the bobbin thread up and hold both threads. Straight-stitch just inside the marked design line.

3   Stitch the entire design. Remove the fabric from the machine and cut the excess batting close to and outside the stitching on the wrong side.

4   Secure a piece of backing fabric or interfacing (large enough to cover the design area) to the wrong side, sandwiching the batting. Baste the layers together. Rethread the machine with decorative thread.

5   With right side up, stitch over the original stitch-ing lines. This stitching is permanent, so be sure to stitch slowly.

6   Immerse the fabric in cool water to dissolve the water-soluble thread. Dry the trapunto flat and block to shape.

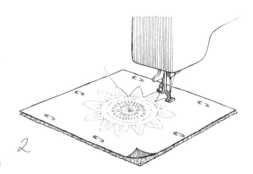

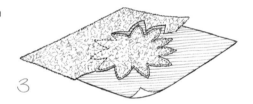

smocking

Smocking by machine is much quicker than smocking by hand—and it looks just as good. Start with a piece of cotton, cotton/polyester, or linen fabric that is two times wider than the desired finished width. The smocking process will reduce the width by half.

Getting Started

Some machines have built-in smocking stitches, but a basic zigzag stitch works just as well. Select the stitches you like and plan how many horizontal rows of stitching you need to fill the desired area. An open-toe presser foot makes it easy to see your stitches. It also travels easily over the fabric folds. Rayon, polyester, cotton, and novelty embroidery thread are good choices.

How to Smock by Machine

1   Thread the machine with water-soluble thread and the bobbin with regular thread. With the wrong side of the fabric up, baste parallel rows of long, straight stitches. Baste the first row $5/8$" (1.5 cm) from the upper edge and baste subsequent rows between $3/8$" (1 cm) and $1/2$" (1.3 cm) apart. Secure the thread tails on one end.

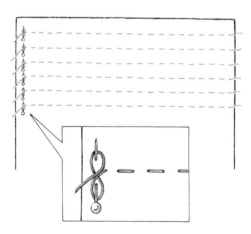

2   Pull the threads on the unsecured end slowly and evenly to form pleats. Secure the pulled threads. Even out the folds with your fingers or a wide-tooth comb.

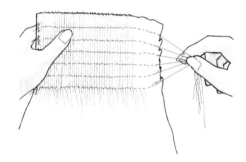

3   Decorative-stitch on the right side, parallel to and between the rows of gathering stitches. Hold the fabric slightly taut so the folds don't shift. Stitch every row in the same direction. Remove the basting stitches.

beads and sequins

Sequins and beads add sparkle, glitz, and color—it's up to you! If you're sewing only a few beads or sequins, it might be just as easy to attach them by hand.

To sew beads and sequins by machine, use a small needle (8/60) and monofilament nylon thread. Hoop the fabric and set your machine for free-motion embroidery. Remove the presser foot, and take several stitches in place to lock the thread.

single beads: Slide a bead onto the tip of the needle and stitch through the hole once. Move the hoop slightly and take a second stitch on one side of the bead. Repeat two or three times in and out of the bead.

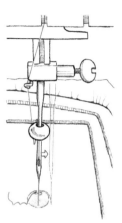

single sequins: Take a stitch to the side of the sequin. Move the hoop and stitch through the center of the sequin. Move the hoop again and take the last stitch on the opposite side from where you started.

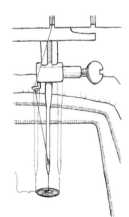

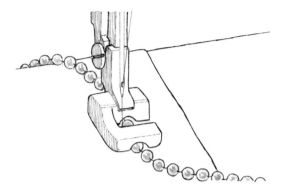

bead and pearl strands: Install a cording foot (see page 7) and couch back and forth over the strand of beads with a zigzag stitch.

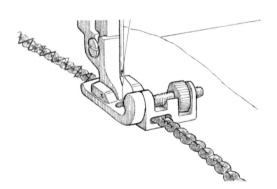

sequin strands: Attach a sequin foot or open-toe presser foot. Align the sequin strand so the sequins slide smoothly under the presser foot. Zigzag-stitch across the sequins without piercing them.

lace insertion

With this heirloom technique, you stitch a strip of lace trim to the right side of the fabric along both edges and trim away the fabric behind the lace. The finished effect is an opening in the fabric that is filled with lace.

Guidelines

- Select lace with two straight, finished edges—designed for insertion.
- Match the weight of the fabric to the lace trim. Choose lightweight, natural-fiber fabrics, such as cotton or linen.
- Install an open-toe or embroidery presser foot (see page 7).
- Prewash the fabric and trim, then press and starch them.

- Mark a placement line with a water-soluble fabric-marking pen.
- Pin or baste water-soluble or tear-away stabilizer to the wrong side of the fabric, behind the placement line.
- Straight-stitch, narrow-zigzag, or hemstitch (see page 54) the lace in place.

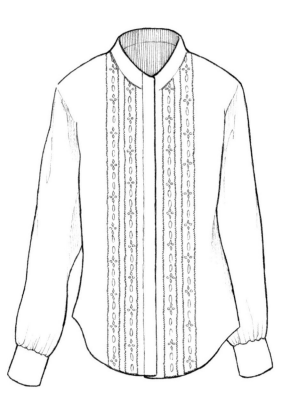

How to Insert Lace Trim

1 Pin the lace to the right side of the fabric, aligning the midline of the lace along the marked placement line. Stitch one edge of the lace, then the other, working in the same direction.

2 Remove the stabilizer and cut through the fabric between the two rows of stitching. Do not cut through the lace. Press the edges of the fabric to each side.

3 Narrow-zigzag or change to a single-wing needle and hemstitch (see page 36) on the right side of the fabric, parallel to each edge of the trim. Trim excess fabric on the wrong side, close to stitching.

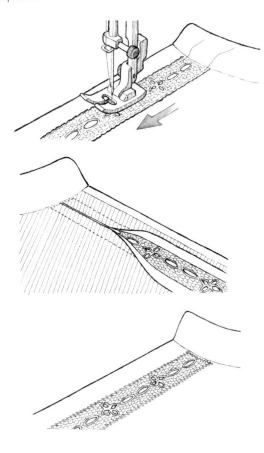

fagoting

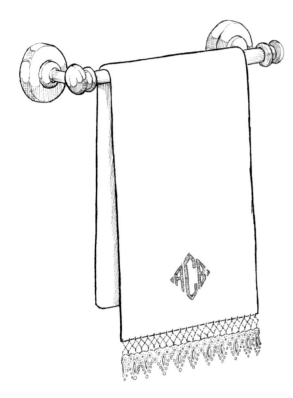

Fagoting is a technique for joining two finished edges with a decorative stitch, leaving a gap between the edges. The decorative opening is especially nice as a border design. Make a test sample on scrap fabric first.

Guidelines

• Experiment with the decorative stitches on your machine. Some machines have specific fagoting stitches, but any stitch that has a back-and-forth motion will work, including zigzag, feather, and honeycomb stitches.

• Match the thread with the weight of the fabric. Cotton or rayon embroidery thread is a popular choice. Choose topstitching thread for heavyweight fabrics.

• Loosen the needle tension slightly.

• Finish and spray-starch the edges of the fabric and/or trim that you are joining.

• Install an open-toe or embroidery presser foot (see page 7).

How to Fagot-Stitch

1   Baste water-soluble stabilizer on the wrong side so the two fabric edges are about ¹/₈" (3 mm) apart. The stabilizer keeps the opening the same width throughout the stitching.

2   Set the machine for a wide decorative stitch Place the stabilized fabrics under the presser foot so the needle is in the center of the opening. Stitch slowly, allowing the stitch to catch one folded edge and then the other, spanning the opening.

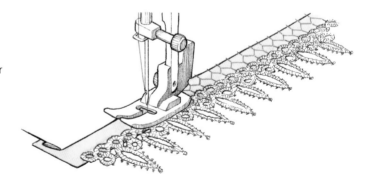

3   When the stitching is complete, remove the stabilizer.

hemstitching

Hemstitching is a classic heirloom technique that features parallel rows of decorative stitching with lacelike holes. You will need a wing needle to create this special openwork effect.

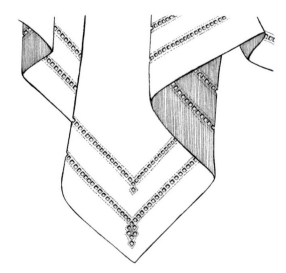

Guidelines

- Choose crisp, delicate fabrics, such as linen and organdy. The fabric must be slightly loosely woven so the needle can separate the threads.
- Prewash the fabric if the finished item will be washed by machine.
- Choose cotton or rayon machine embroidery thread.
- Stiffen the fabric with spray starch and press to minimize puckering.
- Apply water-soluble stabilizer to hold the fabric taut.
- Install an open-toe or embroidery presser foot.

Wing Needles

A wing needle has a flange. The flange separates the fabric threads while the thread wraps around the opening to create decorative holes in the fabric. Join rows of zigzag stitching or built-in hemstitches with single wing needles. To join rows of straight stitches, you'll need a twin wing needle, which has one regular and one wing needle.

How to Hemstitch

1   Mark the stitching line with a water-soluble fabric-marking pen. Install the wing needle.

2   Stitch a row of zigzag stitches (or decorative stitches) along the marked line. Stop at the end of the row, but leave the needle down.

3   Turn the fabric 180 degrees. Stitch back over the previous stitches so that the swing of the needle starts a new row, and the next swing enters a hole of the previous row. Repeat these steps to create a new row of stitching as many times as you want.

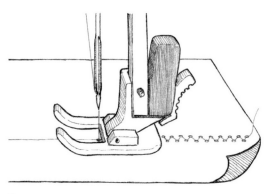

2

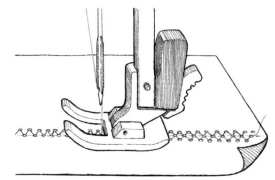

3

pintucks

Pintucks are tiny folds of fabric that are stitched in place. They're usually worked in parallel rows to create texture. You can sew tucks quickly with a pintuck presser foot (see page 7) and a twin needle (see page 8). Or, stitch them traditionally with a zipper foot.

Sewing with a Pintuck Presser Foot

1   Mark the center pintuck with a fabric-marking pen. Position the center of the presser foot over the marked line. Stitch.

2   After completing the tuck, turn the fabric around and place the first tuck into an outer groove on the foot. Stitch the next tuck. Repeat the process on the opposite side of the first tuck, stitching in the same direction.

3   Continue stitching tucks, alternating each side of the center. Stitch two tucks at an equal distance from the center in the same direction. Then change direction for the next set of tucks.

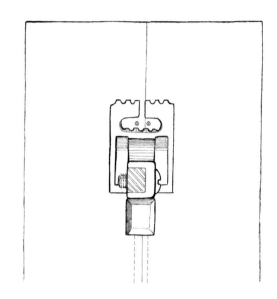

Guidelines

- Work with a No. 2 twin needle for heirloom pintucks (see page 9). The larger the space between the twin needles, the deeper the tuck.

- Thread the machine with two spools of thread, one for each needle. The bobbin thread catches both threads and pulls them together to form the tuck.

- Sew with a straight stitch, between 1.5 and 2 mm long (12 to 16 stitches per inch).

- Increase the needle-thread tension slightly.

- For the smoothest tucks, align the folds along the straight grain of the fabric.

Traditional Pintucks

To sew pintucks with a standard zipper foot, mark a placement line for each tuck, preferably along the grain of the fabric. Fold and press the fabric with the wrong sides together along the placement lines. Stitch 1/16" to 1/8" (1.5 to 3 mm) from the fold, using the edge of the presser foot as a guide. Stitch all the pintucks in the same direction to avoid distorting the fabric.

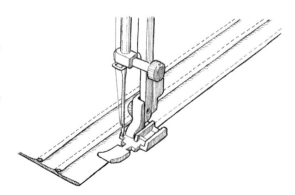

embroidery designs and formats

It's amazing to watch an embroidery machine as it stitches out a design. The machine does all the work. You do the fun part—choosing and editing the design, selecting the thread and fabric, and planning how the project will look! Working with an embroidery machine opens up huge design possibilities—and the learning curve is gentle.

Embroidery Design Formats

Every brand of embroidery machine has its own digital language (which is called its design format). So, any embroidery design you select must be written in the language of your machine.

Designs are built into the machine and available as memory cards issued by the machine's manufacturer. They are automatically in the correct format. You might need to translate designs that are independently published into your machine's language.

This translation process is called format conversion, or reformatting. Work with computer software or a reader/writer box (see page 59) to reformat the design to allow your machine to read and stitch it.

Embroidery Formats

Many designs—whether on memory cards, compact discs (CDs), flash drives, or the Internet—are written in multiple formats and are suitable for many brands of machine. Check the packaging for formatting information. Some of the most common formats include the following:

ART Bernina
EMD Elna & Singer
HUS Viking
JEF Janome
PCD Pfaff
PCM Pfaff (the only machine compatible with an Apple computer)
PEC Baby Lock, Bernina, Brother, Simplicity, White
PES Baby Lock, Bernina, Brother, Simplicity, White
PSW Singer
SEW Elna, Janome, Kenmore
SHV Viking

Built-in Designs

Built-in designs are exclusive to each brand of machine. Most include alphabets, frames, and many other styles of motifs. To work with them, all you have to do is turn on the machine—and, on some machines, attach the embroidery module. Then, with just a touch of the screen, you are ready to stitch any of the many built-in designs. It's that easy! Your owner's manual will show you how to view and stitch each individual design.

Memory Cards

Memory cards fit directly into a slot in the body of the machine. They are brand- or format-specific and hold anywhere from 1 to more than 30 designs. You can buy memory cards full of designs with specific themes—for example, animals, flowers, holiday symbols, sports, and geometric shapes.

When you insert the card into the machine, the machine reads it, displays the stitch information, and stitches the design. These cards are as easy to use as the built-in designs—as long as they are in the correct format for your machine. If a card is not the correct format, convert it with computer software or a reader/writer box (see page 59).

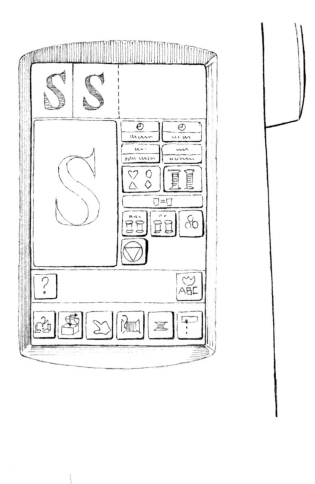

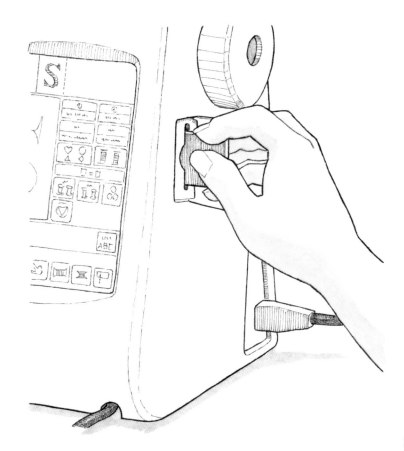

CDs, disks, and the Internet

Thousands of designs are available on CDs, floppy disks, and the Internet. To access these designs, you'll need either a reader/writer box (see page 59) or a computer with machine-embroidery software. Even if you're wary of computers, you'll find this software user-friendly and easy to work with.

CDs and Floppy Disks

Some designs are sold on CDs or floppy disks. A CD holds more information than a floppy disk. Before buying designs on a floppy disk, make sure your computer has a floppy-disk drive, or you won't be able to download the designs. If you need to, you can buy and attach an external floppy-disk drive. Some older embroidery machines have a slot for a CD or a floppy disk that functions just like a memory-card slot (see page 57).

Internet Sources

You'll find countless embroidery designs on the Internet—for purchase or for free! Transferring a design file from the Internet to your computer is called downloading (see page 65). You will need embroidery software for your computer to be able to download and reformat the designs, if needed.

You can simply type "downloadable embroidery designs" into a search engine to find pages of online choices. Many sewing machine manufacturers offer free designs and software on their websites. Independent designers also sell motifs online.

Not all online designs are created equal, however, so test-stitch any design you download from an independent source. You should also protect your computer with virus-scanning software (which you probably have on your computer anyway) to ensure that the design is not infected with a computer virus, which could damage your computer.

Copyright Protection

Embroidery designs and software are copyrighted. When you purchase designs, you are allowed to embroider and adapt them for personal use. In most cases, however, you may not sell the stitched-out designs, even on items that you make yourself. Licensed designs (for example, Disney images) are heavily protected.

You also cannot duplicate software or share it with a friend. In some cases, however, you are allowed to load it onto two or more computers in your own home and/or create a backup copy. Read the documentation that comes with the software and the designs to be sure you understand your rights and restrictions.

the reader/ writer box

Technology makes it possible to work with almost any design in any format in any embroidery machine! A reader/writer box (also called a converter box) reformats designs, so it allows your machine to communicate with external design sources, such as memory cards and your computer.

Reader/Writer Box

A reader/writer box is a format translator. Insert a memory card that's written in a language that your machine can't read. For example, perhaps your machine reads Singer's PSW format and you want to use a memory card written in Viking's SHV format. Insert the SHV memory card into the box. Also insert a blank memory card. The box rewrites the design onto the blank card in the correct format for your machine. A four-slot box has a greater variety of formats then a two-slot box, so it is more versatile. It is also more expensive.

The reader/writer box can also read designs that you have stored on your computer hard drive (which you might have downloaded from the Internet, a floppy disk, or a CD). The box rewrites the designs in your machine's format onto a blank memory card. Then you simply insert the card into your sewing machine to stitch the designs.

The newest reader/writers also let you upload designs onto your computer. With this feature, you can transfer designs from embroidery cards onto your computer. Then, you can edit or combine them with other designs and resave them back onto the memory card. Insert the edited memory card in your machine to embroider your new, modified designs!

editing on the embroidery machine

Many high-end sewing/embroidery machines give you the option of editing a design after you've loaded it into the machine. They usually provide a variety of on-screen editing functions. If your machine has a color touch screen, you can edit designs and preview how they'll look before you stitch them.

Rotating Designs

This function allows you to rotate an entire design, usually in increments of 90 degrees. Some high-end machines rotate in increments as small as 1 degree. You might want to rotate a design so it better fits a specific area. Or you might want to repeat designs at varying angles to get a special effect.

The ability to rotate also helps when you need to hoop a large item. If the bulk of the fabric falls to the right of the needle, rotate the design 180 degrees and hoop the fabric so the bulk is to the left of the needle.

Moving Designs

This basic editing function moves entire motifs anywhere within the stitch field, without changing their shape or proportion. You can shift most designs vertically, horizontally, and diagonally. With this feature, you can also position your stitching at or off center to get the look you want. This function is especially helpful when you're combining several designs on a single hooping.

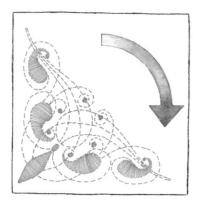
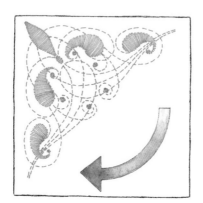
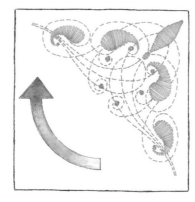
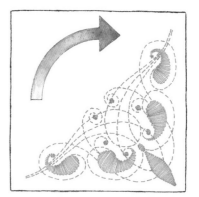

Changing Thread Color

Sometimes you need to change only a few of the colors to create a completely different look. For example, a design in shades of ecru might be very elegant and old-fashioned looking, but the same design in shades of orange might be bold and sassy. Even by changing only one color, you can create an appealing variation.

High-end machines enable you to preview a new color scheme on screen. If your machine doesn't have this feature, stitch the design on scrap fabric first to make sure you like the effect. You can find color-comparison thread charts, and even software, that convert colors from one brand to comparable colors in another.

Color-Stepping

This function allows you to create special effects by not embroidering part of the design. If you set the machine to eliminate one color of a multicolor design, it will automatically skip over those areas. The end result is a more open stitch design, as shown in the drawing below.

With this feature, you can also create an outlined design—perfect if you are making quilting squares. Refer to your owner's manual for instructions. Be sure to make a sample. Sometimes, skipping a color can lead to unexpected results!

 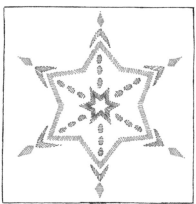  

Combining Designs

With this feature, you can place several individual motifs into the area of a single hoop. From framed monograms to complete scenes, you can build up complex images from an assortment of separate motifs. This editing function also allows you to copy a design multiple times, eliminate a section of a design, and add lettering.

- Test-stitch all the individual motifs you intend to combine.
- Combine the individual stitch-outs to make a template. Doing so allows you to be sure they fit together and also fit within the embroidery area.
- When adding lettering, center the motif above or below the center of the word or phrase.
- If some motifs overlap, work out the order in which they should be stitched. Avoid overlapping too many dense designs.

Resizing Designs

Sometimes, you need to adjust the size of motifs to find a pleasing proportion. This editing function is automatic on some embroidery machines.

When resizing, your main concern is the density of the design. If you make a design larger, but don't add more stitches, it could look sparse. If you reduce a design and don't eliminate some stitches, the design might be difficult to stitch or the stitching might buckle. You can usually enlarge or reduce a design up to 20 percent without affecting the density and the finished look of the design. Some machines automatically adjust the density of designs while resizing them.

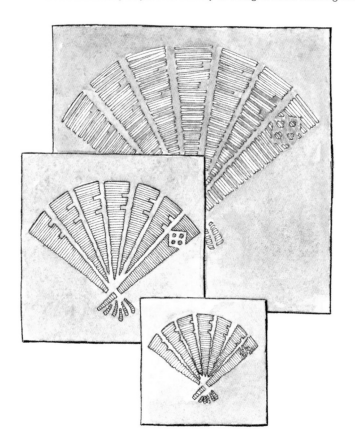

working with your computer

You don't need a personal computer to stitch beautiful machine embroidery—but if you have one, you'll want to use it. It's a terrific tool that will greatly expand the design capabilities of your embroidery machine! It also provides access to the Internet, from which you can download lots of new designs.

Making the Connection

With embroidery software (see page 64), you'll be able to download, view, store, organize, edit, and create original embroidery designs on your computer. You'll also have several ways to move the design from the computer to your embroidery machine.

reader/writer box: This piece of hardware acts as the go-between, or transfer agent, between the computer and the embroidery machine (see page 59).

flash drive: Newer embroidery machines have an outlet, or port, for a flash drive—a small, portable hard drive that stores a lot of information. Plug the flash drive into your computer and copy the design onto it. Remove the drive and plug it into your embroidery machine. Then you can either copy the design into your embroidery machine's memory or stitch it directly from the flash drive.

USB cable: Some machines can be connected to your computer with a cable so you can simply send designs directly from the computer to your embroidery machine.

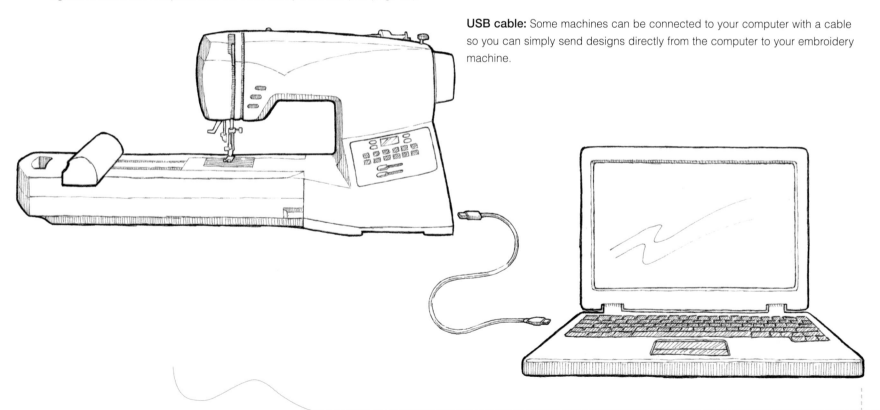

Computer Software

Embroidery software is an essential accessory. The software instructs your computer as to how to reformat, edit, or digitize (translate) machine embroidery designs. Software—on floppy disks, CDs, or the Internet—is constantly updated, refined, and improved, so new products are continually available.

Many software packages are multipurpose. Read the package specifications and system requirements carefully. You might need to add memory or disk space to your computer. Here are some of the most popular types of embroidery software:

conversion software: These programs convert designs from one embroidery format to another.

editing software: Work with this software to customize existing designs. You can cut, copy, and paste areas within a design or combine several designs. Editing software also allows you to rotate, mirror, and center the designs. Most editing programs enable you to change the style of stitches, too.

lettering and monogramming software: With this type of program, you can convert computer type fonts into embroidery fonts and design one-, two-, or three-letter monograms in a variety of styles.

cross-stitch software: Translate images into cross-stitch patterns and convert them to the format you need for your machine.

photograph software: This software converts a black-and-white or color photograph into an embroidery design.

borders and frames software: With these software packages, you can create decorative borders and frames from a large library of graphics. You can also import your own design elements and turn them into a border.

resizing software: Essential for enlarging or reducing the size of a design, this software ensures that changing size won't change the density of the design. It also allows you to change stitch type, length, and direction—and inserts fill stitches as needed.

Modify existing designs with editing or customizing software. Create original designs with digitizing software.

Downloading Designs from the Internet

By logging onto the Internet, you'll have access to thousands of websites that offer digitized software and embroidery designs, ready to stitch. If you've ever purchased anything online, you'll have no trouble learning to download embroidery designs.

Many designs are free. If one catches your eye, simply click on the design (choosing the correct format for your embroidery machine). The design will download to your computer immediately.

If you are purchasing a design, the design is sent to your email address after you provide the necessary information and make payment. Test any design you order online (especially free designs from an unknown or amateur digitizer) on scrap fabric to be sure of its quality.

Create a consistent, easy-to-decipher file-naming system for labelling downloaded design files and any editorial versions you want to save.

How to Download

1   Order a design by clicking on the "download" link and indicate the correct format for your machine.

2   If the design is free, you can open it immediately. If you are purchasing it, the design will be emailed to you. Drag the icon for the design to your desktop to open it.

3   Because embroidery design files are so large, they are usually delivered in a compressed file with the suffix ".zip" at the end of the file name. To open a compressed file, you need expander (or unzip) software. You can find free expander software on the Internet. For computers running the Microsoft platform, download the software called WinZip (www.winzip.com). For Apple computers, download Stuffit (www.stuffit.com). The software includes instructions on how to unzip the file so you can work with it.

4   When you have unzipped the file, open it in your embroidery software program.

5   Edit the design now, if you choose (see pages 60–62).

6   When you are happy with the design, transfer it to your embroidery machine, and stitch.

digitizing images

$\mathcal{D}$igitizing is the process of translating an image into a digital sequence of commands for the embroidery machine. To digitize your own artwork, you need to import it into your computer with a scanner or digital camera. Clip art and images from other sources can be digitized, too, but observe copyright laws (see page 58).

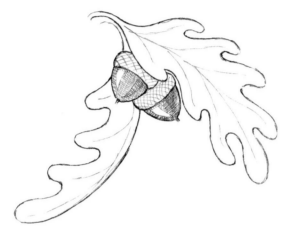

Choosing Software

Most embroidery-machine manufacturers sell their own digitizing software, but there are several generic products that work just as well. If you're confused about which software to buy, consult your machine dealer. They may even offer classes on digitizing.

Because of its growing popularity, digitizing software is becoming easier to use, and many steps are automatic functions. Although you'll still be making the decisions about color changes and stitch types, this software will guide you through much of the process of creating a successful design—so it's worthwhile to learn about all its features and functions. You'll be inspired!

Building a Digitized Motif

To digitize a motif so that it sews out successfully, you need to understand the layers and sequences of stitches that make a design look great. The best way to learn is to watch how your favorite built-in designs stitch out—observe the underlay stitches and the order in which the machine sews the outlines and fills.

Digitizing software helps you create an efficient, attractive stitch sequence that also has the fewest overlaps and jumps possible. You'll need to pay attention to a few things: lock stitches (which keep the thread from unraveling), underlay stitches, types of fill and outline stitches, and the orientation of directional stitches, such as satin stitches. Each detail is important to creating a great design.

Working with Personal Images

You can transform your favorite photographs and artwork into memorable machine embroidery. You only need to upload these images into your computer. Then use your digitizing software to turn them into embroidery. Digital cameras make this process especially easy.

digital cameras: With digital cameras, it's simple to input images into your computer—and, the best part, the images are already in a digital format. You can even photograph your artwork or a fabric pattern and turn it into an embroidery design. Most digital cameras come with a USB cable, which allows you to transfer information from the camera to your computer (see page 63).

Once the image is in your computer, import it into your digitizing software. Then work with the software to transform the images to machine-embroidery designs. When you're ready, transfer the designs to your embroidery machine via a direct cable, reader/writer box, or flash drive (see page 63).

scanners: These freestanding optical devices (either flat-bed or hand-held models) create an electronic version of images or artwork, which you can then save to your computer or onto a memory card.

Some embroidery machines work only with a brand-specific scanner. Others work with a generic scanner. Check your machine manual. Scan the image and import it into your software. Then translate it into stitch commands for the embroidery machine. Again, refer to your manual for specific instructions.

reading the screen display

Each embroidery machine and digitized design comes with certain specifications. It's important to check these out, so you can tell if a design is compatible with the capabilities of your machine and is right for your project.

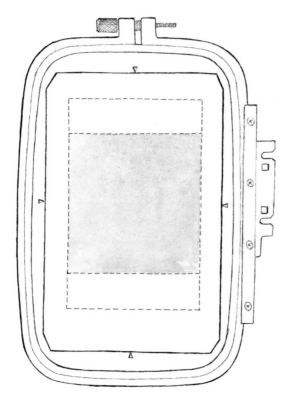

The Embroidery Field

Every embroidery machine has a maximum embroidery field. This field is the largest area that the machine is able to stitch. Know your machine's maximum area before you shop for new designs.

The standard maximum embroidery field is 4" x 4" (10.2 x 10.2 cm; manufacturers and design publishers often refer to this size as 100 x 100 mm). Fortunately, most designs fit within a field of this size. Top-of-the-line machines embroider in a field up to 14" (35.6 cm) in length. Even though the embroidery field is fixed, you can always rehoop and move the fabric to embroider over a larger surface area.

Embroidery Design Data

On machines with built-in designs, the stitch size, total stitch count, and thread-color information appear on screen. You'll also find the information on the packaging of purchased design cards and other types of media.

embroidery size: This feature indicates the actual dimensions of the design, so you can choose a suitable hoop size and position the design on the fabric. It also enables you to estimate how much stabilizer and thread you will need.

stitch count: The stitch counter indicates how many stitches are in the design. This helps you estimate how much thread you will use, how long it will take to stitch the design, and how dense the design will be. Some machines also indicate the estimated stitching time!

thread colors: The list of suggested thread colors helps you plan your thread use. Gather all the threads you need before you start stitching and organize them in the indicated stitching sequence.

selecting a hoop

A machine-embroidery hoop holds your fabric taut. The hoop clips into the machine's embroidery unit, which moves the hoop through the embroidery sequence. Most hoops have an inner and outer ring, with a tightening screw on the outside of the outer ring.

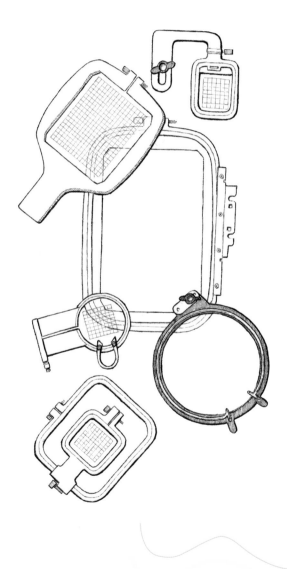

Hoop Size and Shape

Embroidery machines come with at least one embroidery hoop. The standard hoop is 4" x 4" (10 x 10 cm), which is an ideal size for most embroidery designs. A large range of additional hoop sizes and shapes is available for most machines. For the best results, work with the smallest hoop that will accommodate the design—it will hold the fabric more smoothly during embroidery.

You can purchase additional specialty hoops, including multiposition hoops, extra-large hoops, and hoops that will hold baseball caps, socks, cuffs, and other small items. Frame hoops do not have an inner ring because they are for hoopless embroidery (see page 73). Check with your machine dealer to find the hoop options for your machine.

Common Hoop Sizes

Embroidery hoops are labeled with dimensions either in inches or metric units, depending on the manufacturer and place of purchase.

• Standard 4" x 4"	• Standard 10 x 10 cm
• 1" x 2"	• 2 x 6 cm
• 2" x 2"	• 3 x 5 cm
• 2" x 3"	• 4 x 6 cm
• 5" x 7"	• 7 x 7 cm
• 5" x 12"	• 13 x 18 cm
• 6" x 10"	• 13 x 30 cm
• 6" x 14"	• 15 x 24 cm
• 7" x 12"	• 15 x 36 cm
• 8" x 8"	• 16 x 26 cm

positioning the design

To position a design precisely, you need to mark your fabric carefully. The placement guides on the hoop will help with positioning—or you can make your own template. There are a variety of templates, rulers, and boards that will help you stitch exactly where you want. For the most accurate placement, work with special hooping and positioning tools.

Hoop Placement Guides

Most embroidery hoops have placement guides or notches etched directly on the frames, which indicate the horizontal and vertical centers of each side. If guides or notches are hard to see, highlight them with a permanent marker.

Draw a horizontal and vertical line directly on the fabric with a disappearing-ink pen. Position the intersection of these lines at the point where you want the center of the embroidery to be. When you hoop the fabric, align the center markings on the hoop with the intersecting lines.

Placement Templates

To make a placement template, first practice stitching the design on scrap fabric and stabilizer that are similar to the project fabric and stabilizer. (This step is important even if you aren't making a template.) Before you remove the stitched design from the hoop, mark the horizontal and vertical centers on the stitched-out design and trace around the inside of the hoop.

Remove the sample from the hoop and cut around the traced line. Pin the cutout to the fabric, in the position where you want the embroidery to be. Follow the center markings to center it in the hoop. Remove the template and stitch.

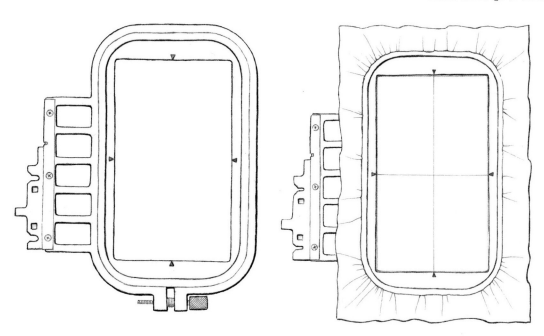

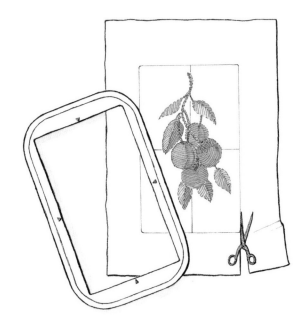

Hoop Templates

Many embroidery hoops come with a template, usually made of transparent plastic, which fits snugly inside the hoop. The template has a hole at the center and notches on each side.

Determine the position of the center of the design on your fabric. Mark the spot with a fabric-marking pen. Place the center of the template at the center mark on the fabric. Mark the side notches on the fabric. Connect the side notch markings with a fabric-marking pen. Refer to those markings to center the fabric in the hoop.

Design Templates

Commercial designs are sometimes packaged with paper or plastic design templates. The templates are printed with the finished design at actual size and include placement markings—which might be, for example, a center opening and vertical and horizontal lines. Place the template on the project fabric and mark the center and side centers. Then align these markings with the hoop's placement guides.

Placement Boards and Rulers

Placement boards and rulers come in many sizes and shapes. They're especially helpful for positioning motifs on clothing. If you plan to embroider on multiple garments, a placement board will make the process much faster and more accurate.

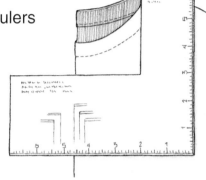

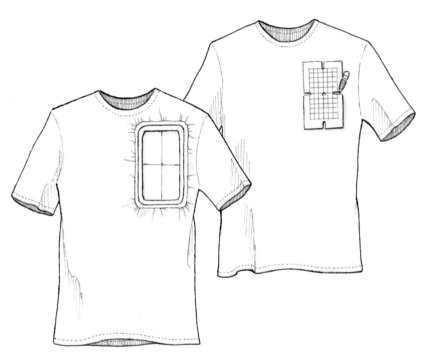

Placement Preview Function

Some machines have "placement preview" and "placement adjustment" features. Placement preview displays the outer boundaries of the embroidery, by moving the hoop through the stitching sequence without stitching. Placement adjustment moves the hoop in tiny increments so you can make sure the needle is exactly where you want it when the machine starts stitching.

how to hoop

After you have chosen a design and positioned it on the fabric, you need to hoop the fabric—preferably the smallest hoop possible. It might take you a couple of tries to get the fabric even and taut. Try not to tug or pull on the fabric afterward. If the surface seems distorted or stretched, remove the fabric and try again.

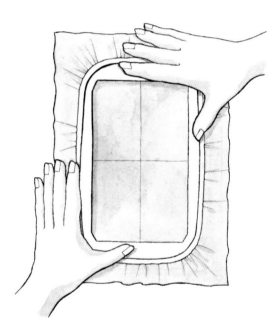

Hooping Fabric

1 Add interfacing (see page 107) to the fabric if needed for your project.

2 Select stabilizer. Decide whether you are hooping the stabilizer and fabric together or just the stabilizer. Proceed accordingly (see page 25).

3 Mark the fabric for design placement.

4 Place the outer hoop on a firm, flat surface. Do not try to hoop fabric on your lap.

5 Loosen the tension screw slightly. Don't tighten the screw after the fabric is hooped.

6 Position the stabilizer alone or the stabilizer and marked fabric (right side up) together over the outer hoop, aligning fabric markings with hoop-placement markings.

7 Lay the inner hoop over the fabric and align markings.

8 With both hands, apply pressure evenly over the hoop until it snaps into place, as shown in the top drawing at left. Keep your hands away from the tension screw.

9 Push the inner hoop slightly below the outer hoop, as shown in the bottom drawing at left, so the fabric rests on the bed of the machine during embroidery.

10 Attach the hoop to the embroidery unit.

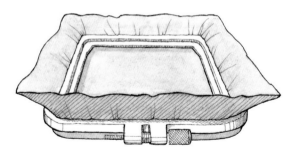

If your hoop stretches out, get a new one. Save the old one for heavier fabrics.

hopeless embroidery

Some fabrics—for example, hard-to-hoop fabrics (toweling, stretchy knits, and fleece) and fabrics that might be damaged by the hoop (velvet and satin)—shouldn't be inserted in hoop frames. Instead, hoop only the stabilizer and attach the fabric to the stabilizer with adhesive. This method is known as hopeless embroidery.

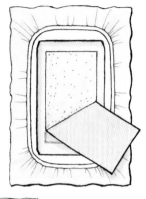

Adhesive-backed Stabilizer

Insert adhesive-backed stabilizer, with the adhesive or paper side up, into the hoop the same way that you would insert fabric (see page 25). For self-adhesive products, score the paper backing inside the hoop and remove it. For water-activated adhesive, dampen the surface of the stabilizer, following manufacturer's directions.

Finger-press and smooth the project fabric, right side up, onto the stabilizer, following the placement techniques on page 25. If necessary, add pins or basting stitches around the edges for extra security.

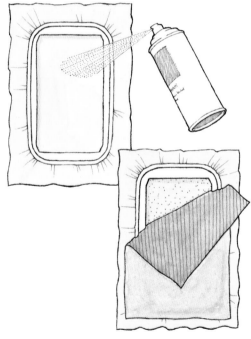

Adhesive Spray

Adhesive spray temporarily holds stabilizer and fabric together. Hoop nonadhesive stabilizer the same way you would hoop fabric (see page 72). Spray the stabilizer, protecting the surface of the hoop with scrap fabric or paper if possible. Finger-press and smooth the fabric or garment onto the stabilizer.

If you are working with a large hoop, wrap the long sides of the inner hoop with athletic prewrap tape or sewing twill tape. The tape helps hold the fabric more securely.

test-stitching

To get the best results, it helps to understand the stitch structure of your design. If you know what the stitches are and how they should look, you'll be able to troubleshoot unexpected goofs. Most designs are made up of three basic stitches.

running or outline stitch: This stitch is good for stitching narrow lines and details, such as the stem of a flower, a letter, or the outline of a motif. This stitch is also used as an underlay stitch, providing a foundation for decorative stitches.

satin stitch: A very tight zigzag stitch, the satin stitch can outline, monogram, appliqué, and fill small design areas, as shown above.

fill stitch: Almost any decorative stitch, including cross-stitch, or seed stitch (shown above), creates texture and fills large areas of a design.

Testing Stabilizer and Stitches

Stitch a test sample with the same or a comparable fabric, stabilizer, and thread. Watch the design stitch out. Then examine the sample for the condition of the fabric, quality of the stitch, and finished effect.

- Change the stabilizer if the fabric puckers, the embroidery feels too stiff, or if the stabilizer is too difficult to remove.
- Adjust the tension if the stitches aren't smooth, the bobbin thread shows on the right side, or the thread forms loops on the wrong side.
- Change thread colors if you don't like the look of the embroidered design.

Testing Tension

If your stitching puckers or forms thread loops on the surface of the fabric, the upper thread tension is probably too tight. If you notice looped threads on the wrong side of the fabric, the upper thread tension is probably too loose. Adjust tension, and if that doesn't help, try this.

- Rethread the machine.
- Remove the bobbin and insert it again.
- Check that the needle isn't worn or damaged.
- Check that there is no lint between the tension discs or around the bobbin case.
- Switch from a horizontal to a vertical spool pin, or vice versa. Tension problems are sometimes caused by the way the thread feeds off the spool.

embroidering, step by step

These basic steps for hooped machine embroidery work with just about any type of embroidery machine. You'll find more detailed information throughout the book—check the index if you need a review. Some cross references are included here.

1 Choose a design and load it into the machine. Adapt, edit, or customize the design on screen (see pages 60–62).

2 Organize your threads. Thread the machine with the first color.

3 Select the appropriate type of stabilizer (see pages 22–24).

4 Mark the design placement on the fabric with a temporary marking pen.

5 Either hoop the fabric and stabilizer together or hoop the stabilizer alone, as needed.

6 Attach or activate the embroidery unit. Attach the hoop to the embroidery unit.

7 Center the needle over the intersecting place-ment lines or center marking. Lower the presser foot. Bring up the bobbin thread and hold both threads as you start to stitch.

8 Follow the prompts on the machine's informa-tion panels for specific instructions.

9 Take several stitches and trim the thread tails. (Some machines do this automatically.)

10 Stitch the first color. When the machine stops, trim any long threads left when the needle is moved from one part of the design to the next (these are called jump stitches).

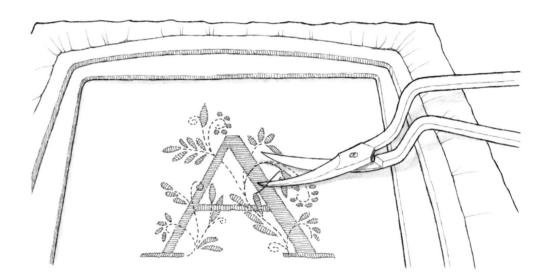

11 To change thread, lift the presser foot. Clip the needle thread at the spool and at the needle. Pull the thread out through the needle. Don't clip the bobbin thread. Thread the machine with the next thread color. Repeat until you have stitched all the colors. Trim any loose threads when you stop to change thread.

12 Check the stitching to make sure there aren't any gaps. If there are gaps or broken stitching, restitch the area before removing the hoop.

13 Remove the hoop from the machine and the fabric from the hoop.

14 Remove the stabilizer and any remaining loose threads. Press the work on the wrong side.

monograms and lettering

Monograms and lettering allow you to add a personal touch to just about everything—from garments to linens to athletic gear. Embroidery machines have several built-in monogram and lettering fonts. You can buy many other styles, too.

Monograms

There are three capital letters in a traditional monogram design. The center letter, which is the initial of the last name, is usually larger than the other two letters. The letter on the left is the initial of the first name. The letter on the right is the initial of the middle name. Single- and two-letter monograms are also popular.

1   Start with a new needle. If the monogram is large and dense (with a lot of satin or other fill stitches), a larger-size needle (80/12 or 90/14) will hold up better.

2   Choose the font (lettering style) from your machine's library of stitches. Program the machine to stitch the monogram, following the instructions for your machine.

3   Thread your machine with the desired type and color thread. Insert a filled bobbin.

4   Mark the design placement on the fabric. Hoop the fabric and appropriate stabilizer. Attach the hoop.

5   Embroider the project. Trim jump threads between letters.

Lettering

Entire words and phrases may already be built into your machine. If so, you can stitch them out as easily as you can stitch a motif.

Your machine has a variety of built-in fonts, which you can work with to spell a name or message. The on-screen editing features help you preview, check, and adjust spacing. You may need to adjust the spacing of the letters so the message is easy to read. Refer to your owner's manual for complete instructions.

borders, corners, and frames

Borders, corner motifs, and frames make dramatic embellishments. You can use built-in motifs, buy designs, or create your own. You might need to rehoop the fabric if your border or frame design is large.

Creating Your Own Border

1. Choose a motif. Make a template by stitching a sample or tracing the design at full scale. Draw a horizontal and vertical line through the center of the motif, as shown in the drawing at right.

2. Working with the template as a guide, draw a vertical positioning line on the fabric that passes through the center of the motif and extends the entire length of the embroidery area, as shown in the drawing at near right.

3. Place the template at one end of the placement line. Mark the fabric with a horizontal line at the center of the motif. Move the template along the vertical line, marking the center of each motif in the same way, as shown in the drawing at far right.

4. Hoop the fabric to fit as many motifs as possible. Stitch, then rehoop as necessary.

Tips for Rehooping

As you embroider large items, you often need to reposition the embroidery hoop. The key to successful rehooping is accurate placement lines.

Hoop the fabric with a large hoop and stitch as many complete repeats as possible. Then raise the needle and remove the hoop. Press out any creases.

Rehoop, matching the placement lines and adjusting the fabric so the needle enters the fabric exactly where you need to stitch the next motif.

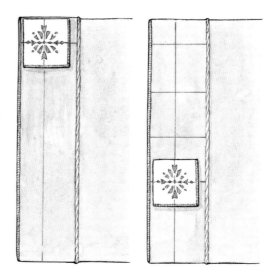

edge finishes

A shaped, embroidered edge adds a couture finish to table and bed linens and clothing. The technique is similar to stitching border designs, except it's done along the edge of the fabric. You may have to seal or trim the outer edge of the embroidery.

Choosing Fabric and Design

Tightly woven fabrics are best suited for edge-finishing. An embroidered edge will look beautiful on both opaque and sheer fabrics.

Edging designs are built into some embroidery machines, but you can buy them, too. The best designs have one satin-stitched edge, which will serve as the finished edge of your project. The design is programmed to automatically repeat units. You may have to rehoop if the edging is longer than the hoop size. Test-stitch the edge design to see how big the repeat is.

Hooping the Fabric

Hoop a piece of tear-away, water-soluble, or iron-away stabilizer (see pages 22–24). Secure the fabric edge to the stabilizer with temporary adhesive spray, as shown in drawing at near right. Reposition the fabric edge as needed so the stitching starts in the right location.

Stitching and Finishing the Edge

1 Thread the machine and attach the embroidery unit. Select or load the desired edge design and start embroidering. You will probably have to stop and rehoop the fabric as you work.

2 After the stitching is complete, remove the fabric from the hoop. Carefully tear, dissolve, or iron away the excess stabilizer.

3 Seal the outer edge of the embroidery with liquid fray preventer. With small, sharp scissors, trim the fabric and any remaining stabilizer close to the stitching, as shown in drawing below at right. If the fabric is a synthetic, you can melt the excess fabric with a soldering iron.

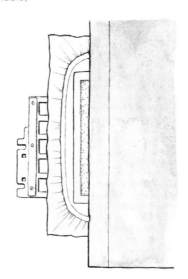

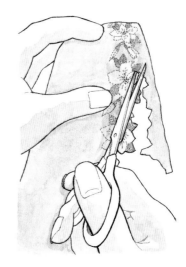

hooped appliqué

Machine-embroidered appliqué is the perfect way to combine fabulous fabric scraps with embroidery. Pull out your fabric stash and get creative with shape, texture, and stitching. Working with your embroidery machine, you can embellish and attach appliqués easily and accurately, in just a few steps.

Fabric and Backing

Tightly woven fabrics are best for appliqué. If you prefer a knit or loose weave, fuse lightweight interfacing to the wrong side first, to prevent the fabrics from stretching during stitching. Avoid fabrics that ravel easily.

If the appliqué fabric is light colored or sheer, back it with a layer of fusible interfacing—especially if you are applying it to a dark background fabric. Always preshrink the appliqué and background fabrics by washing and drying them before starting to stitch.

Appliqué designs won't sag or wrinkle if the appliqué fabric is fused to the background fabric before stitching. Following the manufacturer's instructions, fuse a large piece of paper-backed fusible web to the wrong side of the appliqué fabric. Trace the appliqué shapes onto the paper and cut them out.

The Stitching Process

Hooped appliqué is a three-stitch, three-step process. These steps are preprogrammed for appliqué designs. You simply need to prepare the fabric and stop as needed to attach or trim the appliqué fabric.

1   The outline or guide stitch outlines the perimeter of the appliqué area on the background fabric.

2   The underlay or placement stitch sews the appliqué loosely to the background fabric.

3   The appliqué stitch edges the perimeter of the appliqué with a satin stitch or other decorative stitch, such as the buttonhole stitch.

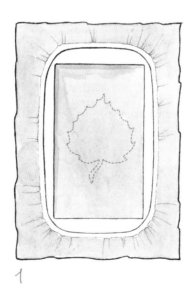

1

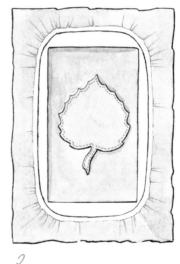

2

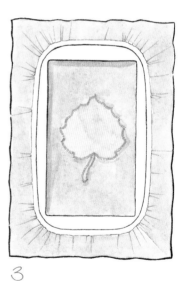

3

appliqué with templates

Many appliqué designs include a template for cutting the appliqué shapes and positioning them on the background fabric. If your design doesn't have a template, it's easy—and helpful—to make one.

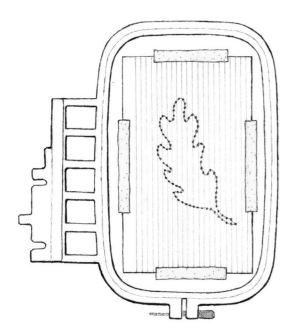

Making a Template

The easiest way to make a template is to tape an index card (or heavy paper, cut to size) to the back of your embroidery hoop (with the inner and outer hoop pieces together). Attach the hoop to the unthreaded machine. Run the outline-stitch part of the appliqué program to perforate the card, as shown in the top drawing at left. Then cut the card on the perforations to create the template.

How to Appliqué with a Template

1 Place the right side of the template on the paper backing of a sheet of fusible web. Trace the appliqué shape. Fuse the web to the wrong side of the appliqué fabric, paper side up.

2 Cut out the appliqué fabric along the traced lines on the paper backing. Peel off the paper backing.

3 Load the design into the threaded embroidery machine.

4 Hoop the stabilized background fabric. Attach the hoop to the machine.

5 Start the embroidery process. Some designs incorporate both embroidery and appliqué in a design. When the machine reaches the appliqué part of the design, it will stitch the outline and stop.

6 Remove the hoop from the machine, but don't take the fabric out of the hoop. Position the appliqué piece and glue it with spray adhesive, or fuse it if you have a small iron that will fit inside the hoop.

7 Reattach the hoop to the machine and continue the embroidering process. The machine will automatically sew the placement stitches and appliqué stitches, as shown in the bottom drawing at left.

8 Repeat the process to stitch any additional appliqué pieces.

9 Remove the hoop from the machine and the fabric from the hoop. Trim the stabilizer and press. Fuse the stabilizer now if you were not able to do so in step 6.

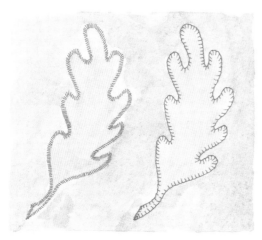

appliqué without templates

If you want to create a more free-form style of appliqué, you don't need an appliqué template. Simply appliqué a piece of fabric and then trim it to the desired shape. Be careful when trimming the excess fabric that you don't cut into the piece.

How to Appliqué without a Template

1 Load the design onto the threaded embroidery machine.

2 Hoop the stabilized background fabric. Attach the hoop to the machine.

3 Start the embroidery process. The machine stops automatically when you need to add the appliqué.

4 Cut a piece of appliqué fabric that is larger than the appliqué shape. Adhere it to the hooped fabric with temporary spray adhesive, without removing the hoop from the machine.

5 Begin embroidering again. The machine will stitch the appliqué outline stitch, then stop. The outline stitch creates the shape of the appliqué and also holds the appliqué fabric to the background fabric, as shown in the top drawing at left.

6 Remove the hoop from the machine, but don't remove the fabric from the hoop. With small, sharp scissors, trim as close as possible to the outline, as shown in the bottom drawing at left. Discard the cut-away fabric.

7 Reattach the hoop and finish with a satin stitch (see page 46) or other decorative stitching.

8 Repeat the process for any additional appliqué pieces.

9 Remove the hoop from the machine and the fabric from the hoop. Trim the stabilizer and press.

Trim the appliqué's excess fabric to within 1/16" (2 mm) of the outline stitches so that raw edges won't show around the finishing stitches.

cutwork

Cutwork is a beautiful heirloom-style embroidery. The design is made by cutting away areas of the background fabric and finishing the cut edges with satin stitches. It's easy to find digitized embroidery motifs designed specifically for cutwork.

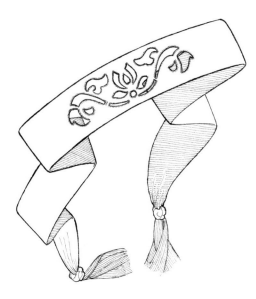

Fabrics and Designs

Work with closely woven fabrics that do not ravel excessively. Lightweight linen and cotton are good choices.

Make a placement template for the design. Test-stitch the design on scrap fabric and stabilizer, working with the same layers you will use in your project.

Shadow cutwork has a dramatic, three-dimensional look. Sandwich a piece of sheer organza or organdy between the fabric and the stabilizer. When you cut out the fabric and remove the stabilizer, the sheer fabric creates a shadow effect.

How to Make Cutwork Embroidery

1 Mark the design placement on the fabric. Hoop the fabric, placing water-soluble stabilizer behind it.

2 Thread the machine and install a bobbin with matching thread. Cotton, rayon, or polyester embroidery thread are excellent choices.

3 Attach the embroidery unit and begin the embroidering process. The machine will stop after stitching a double row of outline stitches.

4 Remove the hoop from the machine, but don't remove the fabric from the hoop. With appliqué scissors, trim the fabric (not the stabilizer) close to the inside row of stitching.

5 Reattach the hoop to the machine and continue embroidering. When the machine is finished, remove the hoop from the machine and the fabric from the hoop. Rinse away the stabilizer.

You may not realize it, but your serger provides many additional ways to embellish fabrics. Sergers, or overlock machines, are capable of much more than simple utilitarian edge-finishing!

Unlike a sewing machine, which stitches with a bobbin thread and a single needle thread, most sergers work with two to five threads—some sergers stitch with as many as eight! The threads run through multiple needles and loopers. The loopers do not pierce the fabric. They work with the needles to wrap thread around the cut fabric edges.

Because the looper threads don't have to fit through the eye of a needle, you can work with just the sort of heavy, textured threads that are perfect for decorative stitching.

Pull out the owner's manual and experiment with your machine's many different thread combinations. You'll be inspired by all it can do!

To explore what your serger can do with decorative thread, make a sampler of serger stitches, taking note of the threading patterns and thread tension.

thread selection

Sergers are the perfect tool for working with heavy, textured decorative threads. You don't have to worry about needle size, because you can thread these threads on the machine's loopers, which don't pierce the fabric. Instead, they wrap the threads around the fabric edge or on top of the fabric surface.

Serging with Decorative Thread

- Practice on scrap fabric to see how the thread behaves and to make any necessary tension adjustments.
- Work with expensive decorative thread only in those areas where the thread will be visible. The thread in the upper looper is usually the most visible thread.

- Thread lightweight, strong, and fray-resistant threads through the needles.
- Increase the stitch length for heavy or textured thread. Test the effect on scrap fabric.

- Cover the thread spool with a special thread net if a thread is slippery and slides or spills off the spool. You can purchase thread nets from your dealer.
- Place a spool cap, supplied with most sergers, over parallel-wound thread so it feeds smoothly. There is a notch cut into most thread spools to hold the thread when it isn't in use. Make sure the notch is on the bottom when you place the thread on the spool pin, so the notch doesn't snag the thread as it unwinds.

- To avoid snags, check the thread tension by pulling each thread, one at a time, above and below the tension dials.
- Create dramatic color and better stitch coverage by passing the fabric edge through the serger twice.
- Blend colors and textures by threading the loopers with several different-colored threads.
- Stitch slowly and check carefully for consistent tension. Adjust the thread tension settings to get the results you want.

A loop-shaped dental-floss threader is handy for threading loopers. Insert the thread through the loop and then pull the threader through the looper.

basic serger stitches

A serger creates a professional-looking edge finish. It sews, trims, and overcasts in one step at a very fast speed—up to 1,600 stitches per minute. Here are some of the most popular utility stitches, which you can use decoratively, too. Refer to your owner's manual for specific settings and instruction.

Two-thread Overedge

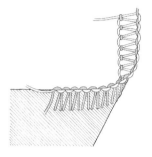

common uses: lightweight edge finishing on woven fabrics
threading: one needle, one looper

Three-thread Overlock

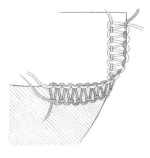

common uses: seaming knit fabrics, edge finishing on woven fabrics
threading: one needle, two loopers

Four-thread Safety

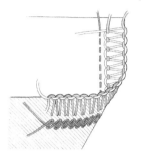

common uses: seaming and overedge stitching in one step; ideal for lightweight woven fabrics
threading: two needles, two loopers

Five-thread Safety

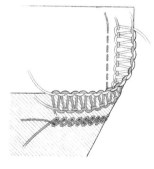

common uses: seaming and overedge stitching in one step on woven fabrics
threading: two needles, three loopers

Rolled Edge/Hem

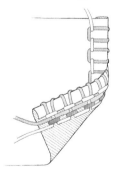

common uses: hemming lightweight fabrics with narrow, dense edgestitching
threading: one needle, one or two loopers

decorative effects

Here are some decorative effects you can create with the serger. Experiment with fancy threads to emphasize the stitches. Disengage the knife blades when stitching away from the fabric edge and when couching trim.

Chain Stitch

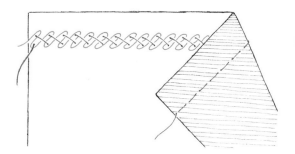

common uses: for seaming and making serger chain trim, work the chain stitch alone or with an overedge stitch (see page 87)
threading: one needle, one looper

Decorative Rolled Edge

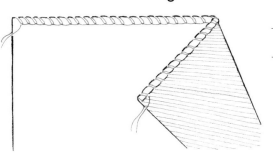

common uses: for decorative hemming and edge-finishing, adjust the tension and stitch length to create a picot or slightly scalloped edge
threading: one needle, one or two loopers

Cover Stitch

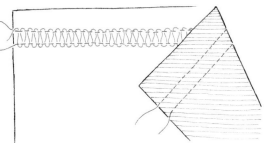

common uses: resembles twin- or triple-needle stitch on the right side and overlock on the wrong side
threading: two or three needles, two loopers

Flatlock Stitch

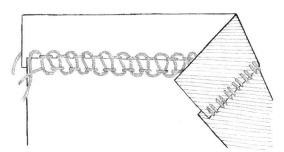

common uses: for seaming, couching, and decorative effects, pull the fabric layers open, loops on one side, ladder on the other
threading: one needle, one or two loopers

Flatlock Couching

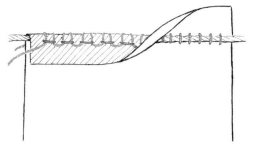

common uses: for decoratively stitching trim or couching material to the fabric, fold the fabric, right sides together, over the couched material, flatlock along the fold, set the machine to the longest stitch, then stitch and unfold the fabric
threading: one needle, one or two loopers

Rolled-hem Pintucks

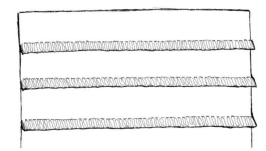

common uses: for heirloom effects, press tucks as for traditional pintucks (see page 55), then stitch a decorative rolled edge along the fold
threading: one needle, two loopers

serger settings

Differential Feed

Differential feed is a machine function that controls the movement of the two sets of feed dogs. One set pushes the fabric under the presser foot from the front. The other set pulls the fabric from behind the presser foot.

Each set works independently, so you can adjust the movement of the front feed dogs to stretch or ease the fabric through the presser foot. Make several small adjustments, rather than one major adjustment. Test the feed on scrap fabric before working on the project fabric.

N (normal) or 1: standard serging for smooth, flat edges on stable fabrics

greater than 1: prevents stretching in knits or gathers lightweight woven fabric

less than 1: stretches lightweight, sheer, and silky fabrics to prevent puckering; creates a decorative "lettuce edge" on knits

Stitch Settings

stitch width: On most sergers, the stitch width is adjusted with a dial that moves the stitch finger and knife blades. On some older or lower-tech sergers, you have to physically change the position of the needle to produces two widths: narrow, for a rolled edge, or standard, for edge-finishing.

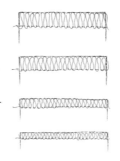

stitch length: Stitch length affects the thread density of the stitch: The shorter the stitch, the greater the density.

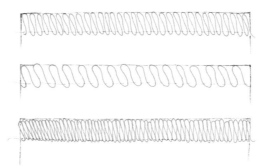

Thread Tension

Most decorative stitching requires you to make some adjustment to the thread tension. The weight of the thread, the thickness of the fabric, and the width/length of the stitches are all factors in the amount of tension you need.

To have balanced tension, the upper and lower looper threads should be the same width. They should meet and also extend just beyond the fabric edge. Once you know how to achieve balanced tension, you can adjust it for any type of specialty stitch. Experiment with different settings to get a feel for it. Computerized sergers have self-adjusting tension.

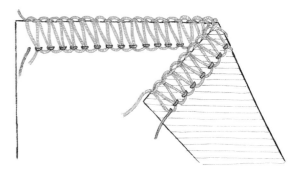

fabric and thread

It's exciting to pick up a needle and thread and, with a few hand stitches, transform something plain into something special. Better yet, these traditional hand-made works of art are portable—so you can work on them anywhere.

Fabric and Thread

Whether you choose to stitch on fabric yardage or a ready-made item, the fabric needs to be firm enough to hold the stitches and supple enough that the needle can go through it. Avoid very loosely woven fabrics. All fabric weights are fine, but if your fabric is lightweight, support it with interfacing or stabilizer (see pages 21–25). Cotton and linen are traditional favorites for hand embroidery.

If you are working with fabric yardage, cut it 2" to 4" (5 to 10 cm) larger all around than the finished piece will be. Cut the fabric edges on the straight grain.

Evenweave fabric is used for counted embroidery stitches like cross-stitch because the fabric threads form a grid. It's appropriate for home décor items, accessories, and samplers.

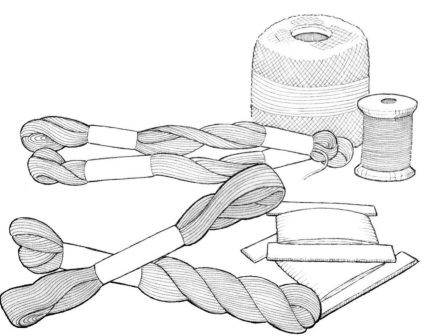

Types of Hand-Embroidery Thread

For the best results, choose thread that matches the weight of the fabric. Fine thread is best for delicate fabrics. Wool or acrylic thread is best for heavier and napped fabrics.

embroidery floss: This cotton thread is made of six strands, loosely twisted together. You can divide it and work with any number of strands.

matte embroidery thread: Heavier than embroidery floss and tightly twisted, matte embroidery thread works well on evenweave fabrics.

crewel yarn: This fine wool or acrylic yarn has a soft, wool-like texture.

flower thread: Flower thread is very fine with a matte finish and is good for tightly woven fabrics.

perle cotton: This heavy, strong, versatile thread has a high sheen.

Persian yarn: This wool or acrylic yarn has three strands, but you can work with one or two if you prefer.

needles and other supplies

You don't need many supplies for hand embroidery. For most projects, you can store everything you need in a sturdy tote bag. Keep the bag handy so you can take it along when you travel or pick it up easily when you have a few quiet minutes at home.

Needles

There are four types of needles for decorative hand stitching. Work with a blunt-tip needle for cross-stitch and sharp-pointed needles for all other types of embroidery. Small, fine needles are fine for lightweight fabrics. You need larger needles for heavier fabrics.

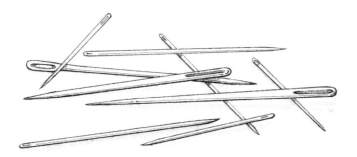

crewel or embroidery needles: These medium-length needles have sharp points and a large eye. They're fine for most types of embroidery.

chenille needles: Chenille needles also have sharp points, but are longer than crewel needles. They also have a larger eye to accommodate heavier fabrics and threads.

tapestry needles: Tapestry needles are thick, with a large eye and a blunt or rounded tip. Choose these when you're stitching evenweave fabrics.

beading needles: The finest of needles, beading needles will fit through the holes of very small beads. They also have a very tiny eye.

Other Supplies

• Embroidery scissors or thread snips

• A thimble, to protect your finger

• A fabric-marking pen or pencil, to copy design lines

• Dressmaker's carbon paper, to transfer designs onto fabric

• A needle threader, for working with heavy thread and yarn

• Masking tape, to bind fabric edges and prevent raveling

• A magnifying glass, to see small stitches and design areas

• Interfacing and/or stabilizer (see pages 21–24), to support the area under the stitching

One great way to learn hand embroidery is with a needlecraft kit. There are many types available. All include a marked background fabric, needle, thread or embroidery floss, and full instructions.

transferring designs to fabric

The first step in hand embroidery is getting the design onto the fabric. You can purchase iron-on design transfers, premarked fabric squares, or needlecraft kits that include fabrics with the design already in place. Or you can create an origianl by drawing directly on the fabric with a fabric-marking pen.

Create designs from your own sketches, a photograph, or a drawing in a book. Omit the fine details as you copy the design. When you find a design you like, enlarge or reduce it with a photocopy machine to get the size you want. There are several techniques for transferring a design onto your project fabric.

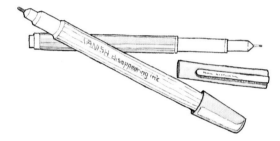

water-soluble fabric-marking pens: Draw your own design lines directly onto the project fabric to guide your stitching. Don't use tailor's chalk or air-erase pens, because they might brush off or disappear before you finish stitching.

iron-on transfer pencil: With these special pencils, you can draw designs on paper, then transfer them to your project by ironing. Be sure to draw designs in reverse.

iron-on transfers: You simply iron these designs directly onto your fabric, following the instructions provided with the transfer. Then you can fill in or outline the design with the suggested stitches or your own favorites.

dressmaker's carbon paper: This product works best on smooth fabric. Light-colored paper is necessary for dark fabrics, and dark-colored paper for light fabrics. Always test the paper on a fabric scrap to make sure it doesn't harm the fabric.

Place the carbon side on the right side of the fabric. Place the design over the carbon paper. Gently trace over the main design lines with a soft lead pencil, taking care not to tear through the paper. The pressure of the pencil transfers carbon onto the fabric.

embroidery hoops and frames

Most hand embroidery is stitched with the fabric secured in a hoop or frame. Taut fabric supports smooth, even stitching. A hoop isn't absolutely necessary on small projects, but it makes it easier to hold the fabric. There are several variations of the two-ring hoop and the stretcher frame. Lap hoops and frames are small and portable. Floor-standing hoops and frames enable you to stitch with both hands.

Stretcher Frames

Stretcher-style frames are best for large pieces, such as wall hangings. They have a roller top and bottom. The fabric is mounted along the top and bottom so that it stretches evenly and without distortion while you're stitching. Some frames snap together for easier mounting.

Hoop Frames

Hoop frames are popular because they are portable, lightweight, and very affordable. They come in many sizes and shapes and are made of wood, plastic, or metal. They have an inner and an outer ring that snap together to hold the fabric taut between them. There's usually a screw on the outer hoop for adjusting the tension for different fabric weights.

Choose a size that fits the embroidery and is comfortable to hold. If the design is larger than the hoop, work one part of the design and then reposition the hoop. Be careful that you don't distort the stitches while rehooping.

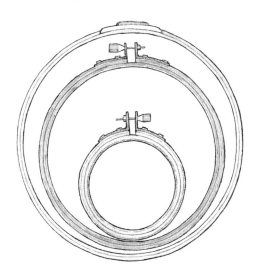

Finding Your Fit

To find the best-size hoop for your hands, place your thumb on the outer ring and stretch your fingers toward the center of the hoop. Your fingers should reach the center of the frame. To determine the best-size frame, place your elbow on the side and stretch your fingers. Again, your fingers should reach the center.

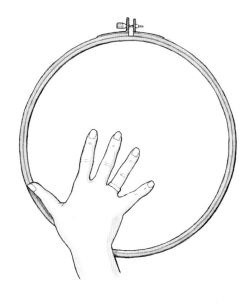

hooping fabric

If you hoop the fabric correctly, you are guaranteed to have comfortable, easy stitching sessions. After you transfer your design, you'll need to bind the fabric edges, prepare your thread, and (if necessary) stabilize the fabric before you're ready to put the fabric in the hoop.

Binding the Fabric Edges

Prevent the fabric edges from fraying by binding them, in one of these four ways:

• Machine-zigzag around the raw edges.

• Turn under 1/2" (1.3 cm) and stitch.

• Fold masking tape over the edges.

• Clean-finish the edges with a serger.

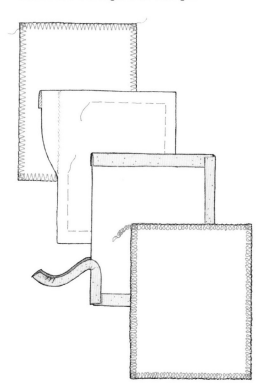

Hooping Fabric

To secure the fabric in the hoop, loosen the screw and separate the rings. Lay the fabric over the inner hoop, with the right side of the fabric facing up. Place the outer ring on top of the inner ring and gently press. You want to be sure that the fabric is smooth and taut and the rings are nested together. Tighten the screw on the outer hoop.

To stretch fabric on a frame, refer to the manufacturer's instructions, because all frames are different.

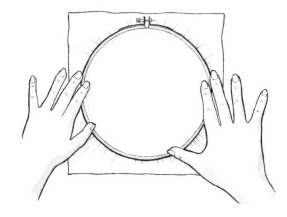

Hooping Small Items

To secure fabric that is too small for a hoop or frame, baste it directly onto a piece of backing fabric (muslin is fine). The backing should be large enough to mount in a hoop or frame. Hoop or frame the backing and then cut away the backing fabric underneath the embroidery area.

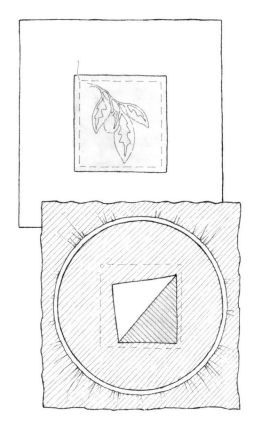

starting and finishing

To help prevent your embroidery from ever unraveling, start and finish it with securing stitches. A few backstitches at the beginning and end of the stitching will usually do the trick. If the project will be worn and laundered frequently, add an end knot for extra security. You'll also want to block the project so it holds its shape.

Starting Stitches

To secure the first thread, work one or two back-stitches (see page 96). Stitch in a spot that will later be covered with decorative stitches, holding the thread tail under the first few stitches.

To secure a new thread color, slide the threaded needle through previous stitches on the wrong side of the work, as shown in the drawing below.

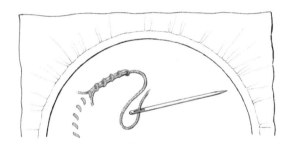

Finishing Stitches

End your stitching with a single backstitch and run the thread tail under previous stitches. When you change thread color frequently within one project, secure both the beginning and ending thread tails.

There are several ways to do this. You can take two or three tiny backstitches, hand-stitch long tails under other stitches, or dab liquid fray preventer at the end of the stitching on the wrong side of the fabric.

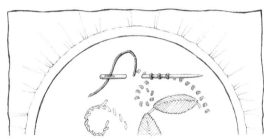

If the thread twists while you are stitch-ing, dangle the needle, and it will spin to untwist the thread naturally.

Blocking the Project

Blocking any needlework project straightens and squares the finished work and also removes any hoop creases. Soak the entire piece in cold water—dip a strand of the same thread in water first to make sure it is colorfast. Remove excess water from the piece by wrapping it in a towel (do not wring or twist it).

Pin the piece to a soft, dense board covered with a towel, so that the corners form 90-degree angles. Gently stretch and pin the sides straight. Let the piece dry. Working with a press cloth, lightly press the wrong side, with the right side face down on a padded surface, such as a clean towel.

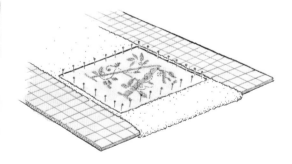

hand-embroidery stitches

Hand-embroidery stitches are so versatile—and there are so many—you can create endless embellishments and special effects. The simple stitches shown here will work beautifully in any type of project. You can find more intricate stitches in books devoted to hand embroidery.

Backstitch

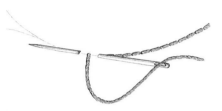

common uses: series of straight stitches for seaming, outlining, filling small, intricate shapes
tip: Work from right to left, keeping stitches between $^1/_8$" and $^1/_4$" (3 and 6 mm) long.

Blanket Stitch

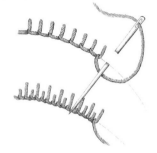

common uses: decorative stitch for edge finishing, appliqué, cutwork, and buttonholes, decorative stitching
tip: Vary the length of the stitches for decorative effects.

Chain Stitch

common uses: series of looped, linked stitches, for outlining or filling an area
tip: Work tiny loops for filling areas, larger or varied sizes for decorative lines.

Cross Stitch

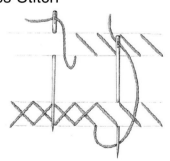

common uses: even-sized x's used to outline and fill spaces, usually worked on evenweave fabric
tip: Work from right to left, then come back from left to righ between parallel guidelines.

Feather Stitch

common uses: decorative stitch used in smocking, crazy quilting, and appliqué
tip: Work from top to bottom between parallel guidelines.

French Knot

common uses: knots worked individually or in clusters, for texture or as a fill stitch
tip: Vary the size of the knot by wrapping the thread around the needle one, two, or three times.

Herringbone Stitch

common uses: decorative stitch often worked along an edge or as a foundation for other stitches
tip: Work from left to right, between parallel guidelines.

Lazy Daisy

common uses: a cluster of individual chain stitches worked from a center point to make a flower shape
tip: Experiment with tension of the loops to create different petal effects.

Running Stitch

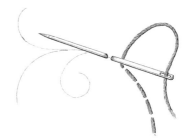

common uses: broken line of stitches for seaming, outlining, and creating foundation for a padded stitch
tip: Work with heavy thread for a bold look.

Satin Stitch

common uses: series of closely spaced stitches for filling areas, often padded for enhanced texture
tip: Keep stitches less than 1" (2.5 cm) long, or they'll snag and look sloppy.

Seed Stitch

common uses: very short, straight stitches for filling areas
tip: Vary the density of the stitches to create different effects.

Stem Stitch

common uses: slightly textured stitch for outlining
tip: Work from left to right over marked guidelines.

Straight Stitch

common uses: individual stitches for filling areas or creating linear shapes
tip: If stitches are widely spaced, knot or backstitch between stitches and trim the thread.

smocking

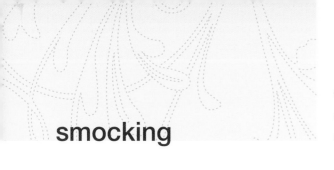

Smocking is the art of embroidering on pleated fabric. You often find it on children's clothing, but smocking has a vintage elegance that looks just as great on dresses, blouses, and other garments (including pirates' shirts, of course!).

Most smocking is done with three strands of embroidery floss, but work with two strands when smocking lightweight fabrics. Work with four to six when working with heavyweight, dark-colored fabrics.

Untwist your embroidery floss periodically by holding the end of the floss and letting the needle drop to the fabric. Untwist the floss as you slide the needle back up toward your fingers. Straight strands will ensure that the stitches lie smooth on the pleats.

Pleating Fabric

Before you can begin smocking, the fabric must be folded into narrow, parallel, perfectly even pleats that run along the grain of the fabric. Preshrink your fabric before pleating.

There are a few ways to pleat fabric. The easiest way is to take the fabric to a tailor and have pleats made professionally. If you prefer to pleat the fabric yourself, mark the pleats with Iron-on Smocking Dots, as shown in the drawing at right, or invest in a pleating machine. Both are sold with complete instructions.

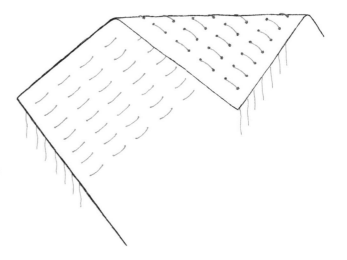

Cable-Stitch Smocking

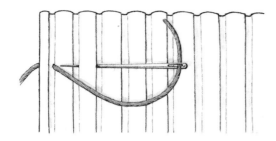

The basic cable stitch anchors the pleats. It is also the basis for several other stitches, such as the wave and the trellis. Work parallel rows of cable stitch across the pleated area, spacing the rows about ¹/₂" (1.3 cm) apart.

Keep your needle parallel to the pleating threads and insert it through only the top third of each pleat fold. Stitch one pleat at a time. Keep the stitches smooth, slightly relaxed, and evenly spaced, not tightly pinched.

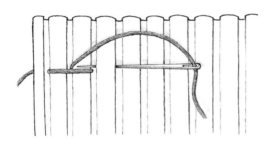

1   Working from left to right, bring the needle to the right side of the fabric, just to the left of the first pleat. Keeping the thread below the needle, slide the needle through the fold of the second pleat from right to left (this is an "under cable"). Pull gently so the stitch is smooth and even.

2   Stitch through the third pleat in the same way, only working with the thread above the needle (this is an "over cable"). Gently pull the thread through.

3   Continue across the row, alternating the thread below and above the needle. Repeat, stitching as many rows as necessary to secure the pleated area. Then remove the original pleating stitches.

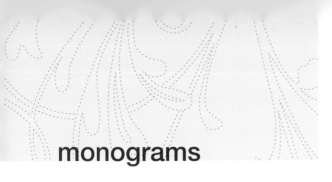

monograms

$Monograms$ $tend$ to go in and out of style for clothing, but they're a classic for home décor items. It's great to know how to stitch them so you can sign the inside of all your original embroidered projects.

Work with any style of alphabet. A monogram usually has three letters, but you might want to stitch a single initial instead—or a favorite saying, school name, or anniversary date. Choose letters and words that are most meaningful to you!

How to Monogram

1 Photocopy an alphabet pattern from a book or pattern, enlarging or reducing the letters as much as you'd like. Transfer the letters to the item you want to monogram.

2 Separate multistrand embroidery floss. Thread two or three strands, cut 18" (45.5 cm) long.

3 Secure stabilizer behind the embroidery area. Insert the fabric in a hoop to keep stitches even and to prevent puckering.

4 Begin stitching by taking two or three back-stitches on the wrong side of the fabric (do not knot). Outline each letter with a chain stitch or stem stitch—or for single lines, an outline stitch (see pages 96–97). To really define the letters and add extra dimension, pad the letters with an underlayer of running stitches, as shown at bottom right.

5 Fill in the letters with cross stitch, satin stitch, chain stitch, or any other stitch you choose, as shown at middle bottom. If the stitches are padded, opt for satin stitches.

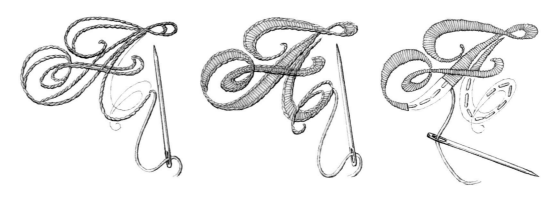

appliqué

Hand appliqué is closely associated with quilting. Various fabric shapes are stitched onto a foundation fabric to create a design or a pictorial image. When the appliqué pieces are small or intricate, hand-stitching gives you the most control. For general appliqué instructions, see pages 45–48.

To keep the appliqué pieces from shifting while you stitch, it's helpful to baste or fuse them in place with fusible web. If the appliquéd piece won't be subject to much wear and tear, you can knot the thread. Otherwise, start and finish the stitching with two or three backstitches (see page 96).

clean-edge appliqué: Cut all the shapes, allowing an extra 1/8" to 1/4" (3 to 6 mm) of fabric around all the edges.

Press under the edges, clipping or notching the raw edges of the appliqué, if necessary, to fold them under neatly.

With invisible thread or a color that matches the appliqué, slipstitch the appliqué to the base fabric. Bring the needle to the right side through the folded edge of the appliqué. Insert it back through the base fabric right next to the folded edge. Continue making small, invisible stitches around all edges.

raw-edge appliqué: If the appliqué fabric is heavy or bulky, it is difficult to turn under the raw edge neatly. Trim the edges or pink them with pinking shears—the pinking also creates a decorative zigzag effect.

Sew the fused or basted piece to the foundation fabric, working around the entire shape, with small straight, chain, herringbone, or stem stitches (see pages 96–97). Secure the stitching with a knot or backstitch.

beads, sequins, and rhinestones

Beads, sequins, gems, and rhinestones add sparkle, color, and style. Scatter them randomly for a hint of glamour or cluster them to form patterns. If you are going to machine-wash the finished project, make sure the embellishment is also machine-washable.

Work with a beading needle and invisible thread (monofilament) or thread that matches the color of the beads. If the beads or jewels are large or heavy, sew tear-away stabilizer beneath them on the wrong side of the fabric.

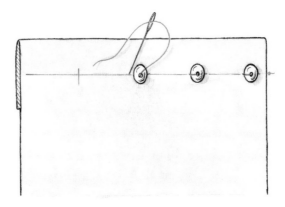

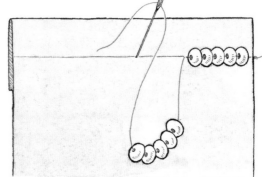

To sew any type of threaded bead trim, lay the trim where you'd like to position it on the fabric. Take a diagonal stitch over the bead's foundation strand, then every three to four beads, wrapping the stitching thread under the beads to conceal it.

single beads: Knot the thread and bring the needle up from the wrong side of the fabric. String a bead on the needle and slide it down the thread to the fabric. Insert the needle back through the fabric, next to the bead. Either knot the thread or sew the next bead.

Repeat until you've sewn all the beads in place. For extra security, take a tiny backstitch every few beads—this way, if one falls off, you won't lose them all!

several beads in a row: Draw a line to mark the bead placement. Knot the thread and bring the needle to the right side of the fabric, on the line. Slide several beads onto the needle, depending on their size. Insert the needle back through the fabric so the beads lie flat.

Bring the needle to the right side of the fabric and repeat until you have attached all the beads. Knot the thread on the wrong side. For extra security, stitch a small backstitch on the wrong side every few beads.

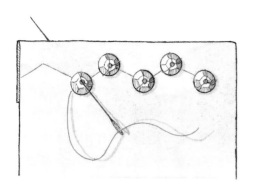
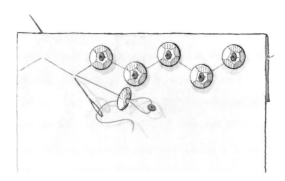
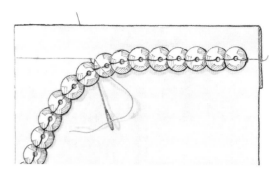

sequins: Knot the thread and bring the needle from the wrong side of the fabric through the hole in the sequin. Carry the thread over the sequin and back through the fabric, right next to the edge of the sequin. Repeat so there are two or more straight stitches holding the sequin in place. Repeat to attach additional sequins or knot the thread on the wrong side.

sequins with seed beads: Knot the thread and bring the needle from the wrong side of the fabric through the hole in the sequin and then through a seed bead. Insert the needle back through the sequin to the wrong side of the fabric, seating the seed bead in the center. Knot the thread end or continue attaching sequins and beads.

prestrung sequins: Draw a line with a fabric-marking pen to mark the desired position of the string of sequins. Lay the string of sequins along the line. Knot the thread and bring the needle to the right side of the fabric, close to one end of the string.

Make diagonal stitches, every three to four sequins, so that the thread travels under the sequins and wraps around the string that connects them. Knot the thread to finish. To prevent fraying, secure the thread ends of the sequin trim with several straight stitches or with a dab of liquid fray preventer.

rhinestones: There are many types of rhinestones. Some types are hand-sewn in place individually, like beads. Others must be glued with fabric glue. One type has a heat-activated backing, so you can apply the rhinestones with an iron or a wandlike heating tool. Another type has a pronged back, so you attach them with a special tool that bends the prongs to grip the fabric. Check the package to determine which application method you need.

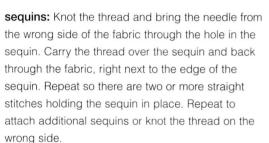
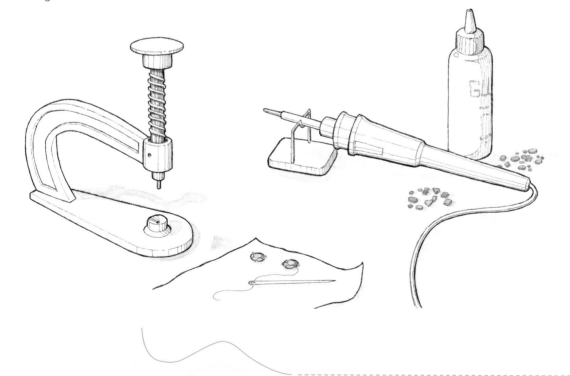

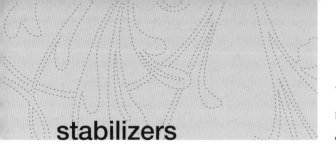

stabilizers

There are many types of stabilizers. You can buy them in precut sheets or on rolls. Keep a selection on hand, but be sure to include at least one sheet of cut-away and one sheet of tear-away stabilizer.

Type	Description	Best Fabrics	Best Techniques	Tips
Cut-away	permanent support, light to heavy weights, adhesive or non-adhesive, good as backing or topping	stretch and stable knits, stretch wovens, loose weaves, denim, corduroy, napped and pile fabrics, leather and suede, vinyl, blanket fabric	embroidery, appliqué, decorative stitching, monogramming, trapunto	Excess is cut away after stitching. Colored or clear plastic/ vinyl sheets work as toppers.
Tear-away	temporary support, light to heavy weights, adhesive, nonadhesive and fusible, good primarily as backing	firmly woven, natural-fiber fabrics (such as linen, cotton, wool), nylon flag fabric, terrycloth	dense embroidery, satin stitching, monograms, appliqués, buttonholes, couching, patchwork, heirloom, edging, decorative lettering	Carefully tear away after stitching. Remove thread whiskers with tweezers
Heat-away	temporary support, light to medium weights, remove by application of heat, good primarily as topping	nonwashable fabrics, delicate fabrics	embroidery, decorative stitching, lace or motif making, cutwork, buttonholes, edge stitching	Cut away as much excess as you can after stitching. Remove with iron. Do not apply steam, always press with a press cloth, and brush away flaky residue.
Water-soluble	temporary support, light to medium weights, available in liquid form, can apply as multiple layers, often used as topping	delicate fabrics, open-weave fabrics, sheers, laces, topping for napped and pile fabrics	open-stitch designs, appliqué, embroidery, cutwork, heirloom, fagoting, smocking, shadow work, lace making, edge stitching	Remove with water by steaming, spraying, or submerging. Store in sealed plastic bag. Repeat applications of water to remove all traces, if necessary.

quick fixes

The most important—and most effective—way to avoid trouble is this: Make a test sample on scrap fabric. This way you can solve design glitches or stitching mishaps before you begin to embroider the actual item or an expensive fabric.

Stitching Problems

If you aren't satisfied with the test sample, try these quick checks:

• Rethread the machine.

• Reinsert the bobbin.

• If the bobbin thread shows on right side, use lighter-weight bobbin thread.

• Clean lint from the bobbin area.

• Remove and reattach the embroidery unit.

• Insert a new needle, making sure it is the right type and size.

• Loosen the upper tension slightly.

• Stitch more slowly.

• Make sure the fabric and stabilizer are secure.

• Clean the needle if there is any adhesive residue.

Puckering and Distortion

If an embroidered motif puckers or is distorted, here are some possible solutions:

• The design is probably too dense for the fabric. Edit the design to decrease the stitch density.

• The fabric might be stretched too tightly in the hoop. Loosen it slightly.

• Try a heavier backing stabilizer.

• Loosen the thread tension slightly.

• Work with a finer thread to decrease the stitch density.

• Rethread the machine.

Breaking or Fraying Thread

If the thread snaps, catches, frays, snags, or shreds while you're stitching, follow these steps:

• Rethread the machine, making sure the thread is not caught in any of the thread guides.

• Be sure that you've installed the right size needle.

• If thread is fraying, switch to a needle with a larger eye.

• Loosen the top tension slightly.

• Clean the bobbin area and tension disks.

• Turn the spool pin around so the thread feeds in the opposite direction.

• Consider buying a larger spool of thread. Thread feeds more smoothly from larger spools.

• Switch from a horizontal to vertical spool pin, or vice versa. Sometimes, the thread gets tangled around a vertical spool pin, or it may spin off a horizontal pin too fast.

• Consider investing in a freestanding thread holder, which includes both horizontal and vertical spool pins (see page 13).

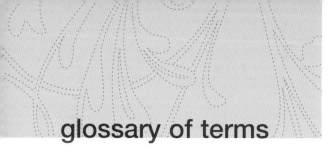

glossary of terms

Decorative-stitching machines and techniques have their own vocabulary. Here are some of the words you'll need to know.

Backing: a stabilizer that is positioned on the wrong side of the fabric (see also stabilizer)

Basting: large running stitches made by hand or machine to temporarily hold together fabric layers or fabric and trim

Blank: a ready-made item created specifically for machine embroidery

Bobbin: a small spool that holds the lower stitching threads, located under the bed of the sewing machine

CD, or compact disc: a digital disk that contains digitized embroidery designs, which can be "read" by your home computer or a converter box

Color stepping: the process of skipping selected colors in a digitized, multicolor embroidery design

Conversion software: computer software that translates embroidery designs into different formats, suitable for different embroidery machines

Converter box: see reader/writer box

Copyright: legal protection for intellectual property, including embroidery designs and software

Cupping: a distortion of fabric, in which the fabric curls or cups around an embroidered motif

Custom designs: original designs that you can create yourself with digitizing software, or that you can have made for you

Customizing: the process of changing or adapting an existing embroidery design, usually with special customizing software (see also editing)

Decorative stitches: any linear stitches other than the straight stitch featured on a sewing machine

Density: the number of stitches per unit of area in an embroidered design

Design size: the dimensions or the finished size of a specific design

Digitizing: the process of transforming artwork from any source, including original drawings, into a digital language for a computerized embroidery machine to read and stitch out with special software

Digitizing software: computer software that enables you to transform any image into a digital format that can be "read" by an embroidery machine

Downloading: the process of retrieving a design from the Internet and transferring it to your computer, a converter box, and/or your embroidery machine

Editing: altering, moving, flipping, or redesigning a machine embroidery design by means of functions on your embroidery machine or special software (see also customizing)

Embroidery card: see memory card

Evenweave fabric: a type of fabric, suitable for cross-stitch, that has the same number of warp threads (the threads that travel parallel to the selvage) and weft threads (the threads that travel perpendicular to the selvage) per square inch (centimeter)

Fill stitches: a series of stitches that repeat to cover or fill in a large area with embroidery

Finishing: the process of completing an embroidery, which includes trimming loose threads; removing excess stabilizer; and pressing, blocking, or steaming the fabric to straighten it and remove puckers

Flash drive: portable, digital medium convenient for transferring embroidery designs from a computer to an embroidery machine

Format: the digital "language" that an embroidery machine "reads," which allows it to stitch machine-embroidery designs

Fusible web: two-sided fusing film that adheres two pieces of fabric (or fabric and trim) by ironing rather than sewing

Hardware: refers to all types of digital equipment, including computer, sewing/embroidery machine, converter box, and other external units, such as a photo scanner

Heirloom sewing: traditional decorative stitching techniques, often worked on lightweight fabrics (such as cotton and linen), in pastel or neutral thread colors; includes pintucking, lace insertion, smocking, and fagoting

Hooping: the process of securing fabric in an embroidery hoop to keep it taut during the process of hand- and machine-embroidering

Interfacing: specialty fabric that is basted or fused to the wrong side of the project fabric to form an additional layer that adds body and stability

Jump stitch: a long stitch that extends from the end of one design section to the beginning of another; must be trimmed away after the embroidery is complete

Linear stitches: see decorative stitches

Lock stitches: two or three small stitches taken at the beginning or end of machine stitching to prevent the stitches from pulling out

Maximum embroidery area: the largest area within which an embroidery machine can stitch

Memory card: a small electronic card—which is inserted into the embroidery machine—that contains digitized embroidery designs

Motif: a single unit of an embroidery design

On-screen editing: the process of editing the various functions of the embroidery machine with a touch screen on the body of the machine

Puckering: the formation of wrinkles in the fabric surrounding an embroidered design, often caused by improper hooping or stabilization

Reader/writer box (also called a converter box): hardware that reads embroidery designs in one format and converts them to a different format

Resizing: a software or embroidery machine feature that allows you to change the size of an embroidery design

Sampler: a piece of embroidery, worked by hand or machine, to test or practice a variety of stitches

Scanner: an electronic device that converts artwork into a digital format so it can be loaded onto your computer, digitized, transferred to your embroidery machine, and stitched

Stabilizer: woven or nonwoven material that supports and stiffens fabric for embroidery and decorative stitching; can be placed on the wrong side of the fabric as backing or on the right side as a topping

Stitch count: the total number of stitches in a machine-embroidery design, determining the design's density, the amount of thread needed, and the amount of time needed for stitching

Stitch out: a completely stitched embroidery design; also the process of creating a completely stitched design

Stock designs: commercially available machine-embroidery designs

Template: a full-scale version of an embroidery design (either printed on paper or clear plastic, or stitched out on fabric), marked with horizontal and vertical centers to ensure precise placement of the design on the project

Test sample: a completely stitched-out design on the same or similar fabric as the project fabric, to check that the stabilizer, thread type, and thread tension are correct

Thread tension: tautness or looseness of the machine's threads as they interlock and form stitches

Topping: a stabilizer that is positioned on the right side of the project fabric, especially fabrics with nap or pile (see also stabilizer)

Underlay stitches: stitches that are sewn in an area that will later be filled with embroidery stitches, to help stabilize the fabric and increase the density and dimension of the decorative stitching

index

A

adhesive-backed stabilizer, 73

adhesive spray, 25, 73

analogous colors, 34

appliqués

    hand, 101

    hooped, 81

    planning and making, 45

    satin-stitch, 46–47

    specialty, 48

    with templates, 82

    without template, 83

appliqué scissors, 12

B

backing, 22

backstitch, 96

balance, 33

beading needles, 91

beads, 51, 102

blanket stitch, 96

blocking, 95

bobbin case, 13

bobbin thread, 20

bobbin work, 39

borders, 77

braiding foot, 7

built-in designs, 57, 68

built-in stitches, 36

C

cable-stitch smocking, 99

carbon paper, 92

CDs, 58

chain stitch, 88, 96

chalk wedge, 11

chenille needles, 91

color, 32, 34, 61

color-stepping, 61

color wheel, 34

complementary colors, 34

composition, 32

computerized sewing machines, 38

computers, 63–67

computer software, 58, 63–64, 66

converter box, 59, 63

copyright protection, 58, 66

cording foot, 7

corners, 77

cotton thread, 18, 20

couching, 42–43

cover stitch, 88

crewel needles, 91

cross stitch, 96

custom stitches, 38

cut-away stabilizers, 23, 104

cutting tools, 12

cutwork, 84

D

decorative effects, with serger, 88

decorative rolled edge, 88

decorative stitching. *See* stitching

density, fabric and stitch, 14–15

design data, 68

design elements, 32

design ideas, sources of, 31

designs

    See also motifs

    appliqués, 45–48, 82–83

    built-in, 57, 68

    on CDs and disks, 58

    combining, 62

    computers and, 58, 63–65

    copyright protection for, 58

    creating original, 33

    drawing, 33

    editing, 60–62

    formats, 56

    Internet sources for, 58, 65

    moving, 60

    positioning, 35, 70–71

    resizing, 62

    rotating, 60

    transferring to fabric, 92

    translation of, with reader/writer box, 59

    trapunto, 49

    using stitch samplers, 36

    working with existing, 32

design templates, 71

differential feed, 89

digital cameras, 67

digitizing images, 66–67

distortion, 105

E

edges

    decorative rolled, 88

    finishes for, 78